The Search
for Ancient
China

‘I am the first sovereign emperor; the generations that will follow me will call themselves the second generation, the third generation, and will go on to a thousand and ten thousand generations, endlessly passing on this principle.’

Sima Qian,
Historical Records,
1st century BC

JAN 2 5 200

CONTENTS

THE SEARCH FOR
ANCIENT CHINA

Corinne Debaine-Francfort

DISCOVERIES®
HARRY N. ABRAMS, INC., PUBLISHERS

The history of China dates back over several millennia, making it the world's longest continuous civilization. It is probably for this reason that this country has such an original and intimate relationship with its past. Yet archaeology, as a modern science of field research, only appeared quite late, in the 1920s and through a series of short cuts.

CHAPTER 1

BIRTH OF ARCHAEOLOGY IN CHINA

For a long time, Anyang (opposite) was the oldest-known historical site. Chinese archaeology made it one of its most vibrant symbols, that of the heart of China, where 'the past is a guide for the present' (quotation from Mao Zedong, right).

A civilization of the written word, a taste for antiquities

Since ancient times, the past in China has been linked with the present. It is a guide from which information can be obtained, a tool that has a hold over space and time, providing models which can be imitated and from which lessons can be drawn. It is also a major source of inspiration.

Writing, an instrument of memory, is one of the main contributions of Chinese civilization. Long before the modern era, the love of antiquities was combined with a taste for texts. From a very early age, ancient objects discovered by chance or hoarded were passed around and preserved. In these early times, texts also related the discoveries of archaic inscribed bronzes, and mentioned or described ancient monuments. Sima Qian, the famous historian at the court of the Western Han, visited many of them. Around 100 BC he recorded the reliable information in his *Shiji* (*Historical Records*).

The appreciation of antiquities is an art cultivated by cultured people. Under the Ming (1368–1644) people were often depicted surrounded by their favourite objects, or studying their collection (painting above).

In his *Historical Records*, Sima Qian (portrait, left) tells the story of the famous tomb of Qin Shi Huangdi, the first emperor of China, and gives a fabulous description of it. Archaeologists have not yet been able to verify his account, as no excavations have been carried out to date.

A carefully listed cultural heritage

Under the Song dynasty (960–1279), the political uncertainties of the time favoured a return to the values of the past, which was defined as a golden age. The cultural heritage was put into different classifications. The antiquities that had been unearthed here and there by peasants were successfully categorized in this way. In the 12th century the emperor Huizong, who was keen to enrich his collections, had test pits dug at the site of Anyang, the last Shang capital of the 14th to 11th centuries BC. Treatises were written that stressed the importance of ancient objects as guides for the future. Descriptive catalogues of antiquities and of inscriptions on stone and bronze were compiled. The most famous is the *Kaogu tu* (*An Illustrated Study of Ancient Things*) by Lü Dalin, dating from the year 1092. It brought together two hundred and eleven bronzes and thirteen jades from the imperial palace and private collections in its ten volumes.

Yet these learned works were abandoned by the Song's Mongol successors. It was not until the end of the 17th century that these antiquities were studied again. However, this was still a very long way from field archaeology: rather more than the remains themselves it was

Like the *Kaogu tu*, the *Bogotulu* (below), published in 1123, is a catalogue of the antiquities collection of the Song court. Each piece is illustrated and identified by its place of

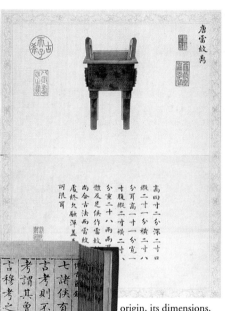

origin, its dimensions, its weight, its inscriptions and its decoration. Most of the inventoried objects were later lost. The album *Xiangye huaying* (*Splendours of Auspicious Metallurgy*), dating from the 18th century, is presented in the same way. Above: watercolour plate of an ancient bronze from the album.

C. T. LOO & CO

ART ANCIEN DE CHINE

PARIS
34, Rue Taitbout

NEW-YORK
559, Fifth Avenue

their inscriptions that the scholars prized.

In the 19th century a vast antiquities market developed, both in China and abroad.

Tradition and modernity, a meeting of East and West

As China opened its doors to western diplomats, traders and clerics, because of the peace treaties signed in Beijing in 1860, a current of xenophobia inevitably developed, not only in popular circles but also among the Manchurian rulers and the old traditional Chinese society, which was convinced of its superiority over the 'barbarians'. However, this enforced opening of its borders, along with western pressure on the margins of the empire, helped new ideas to blossom. From 1870 a great effort was made to train young Chinese in modern archaeological methods. Students in China were taught by foreign specialists. Others were sent to the United States, England and France, and later also to Japan.

It was in this context – troubled times that were nevertheless favourable to new ideas – that modern archaeology took its first steps in China. Its history reflects the contradictions of the period, and its search for identity. During this period there was a meeting between ancient and modern, between textual scholars and field workers and between China and the West.

Edouard Chavannes: a Sinologist in the field

Sinology was flourishing, especially in France where the School of Oriental Languages and the Collège de France trained scholars of the very highest calibre. Some of them, through the texts they translated or the manuscripts they

The great collector and dealer in antiquities, C. T. Loo (left), who had offices in all the great capitals of the world, made westerners familiar with Chinese art.

collected, built bridges between western orientalism and Chinese scholarship.

In this respect, Edouard Chavannes (1865–1918) was a multi-talented forerunner. It is to him that we owe the translation of Sima Qian's *Historical Records*, whose importance for China is comparable to the work of Herodotus for the West.

Edouard Chavannes (opposite bottom) wrote that archaeology 'will not be able to develop fully until methodical excavations have taught us what lies hidden in the depths of the ground'. Yet his contribution to the study of Han monuments (206 BC–AD 220) – the oldest known at that time (below, a funerary column) – was nevertheless essential. Left: the tumulus of Qin Shi Huangdi, who died in 210 BC.

In 1908, continuing in the field his travels in the texts, he returned from China with a precious inventory of funerary and Buddhist monuments, and translated their inscriptions. Thanks to him, the West discovered a heritage of which it had hitherto been totally ignorant.

KAZAKHSTAN

MONGOLIA

INNER
MONGOLIA

15 •

14 •

Tarim

16 • Lop Nor

17 •

GANSU

18 •

XINJIANG

19 •
20 •

Taklamakan Desert

12 • • 13

• 21

QINGHAI

TIBET

SICHUAN

NEPAL

BHUTAN

INDIA

YUNNAN

INDIA

BANGLADESH

BURMA

0

300 miles

0

500 km

Anyang (36)
Banpo (31)
Banshan (21)
Baoji (23)
Beijing (4)
Canton (62)
Chang'an (30)
Changsha (59)
Chengziyai (10)
Chifeng (1)
Cishan (35)
Dahecun (38)
Dawenkou (11)
Dongshanzui (3)
Dunhuang (17)
Erligang (37)
Erlitou (39)
Fanshan (47)
Fengxiang (24)
Fufeng (28)
Gaocheng (9)
Hangzhou (48)
Hemudu (49)
Hougang (34)
Houma (32)
Jiangling (55)
Khotan (12)
Kucha (14)
Leigudun (51)
Liangzhu (46)
Lintong (26)
Liuwan (19)
Liyu (7)
Loulan (16)
Luoyang (40)
Machang (20)
Majiayao (22)
Mancheng (6)
Mawangdui (57)
Nanjing (43)
Ningxiang (58)
Niuheliang (2)
Niya (13)
Panlongcheng (53)
Pingshan (8)
Qishan (27)
Qucun (33)
Sanmenxia (42)
Sanxingdui (54)
Shanghai (45)
Shangcunling (41)
Shizhaishan (61)
Sidun (44)
Turfan (15)
Wucheng (56)
Wuwei (18)
Xi'an (29)
Xianyang (25)
Xichuan (50)
Xin'gan (60)
Xinyang (52)
Zhengzhou (37)
Zhoukoudian (5)

An archaeologist-poet, Victor Segalen

In 1914 Victor Segalen (1878–1919), a poet in search of adventure who had become the personal physician of the son of President Yuan Shikai, discovered a power in great Chinese statuary that reminded him of the megaliths of his Breton childhood. Accompanied by his friend, the writer Auguste Gilbert de Voisins,

•I had the good fortune to find the oldest stone statue of a horse that has ever been discovered in China.• Thanks to this 'horse crushing a Barbarian' described in the *Provincial Annals* of Shaanxi, which provided the plan (above), Segalen was able to identify the tomb of General Huo Qubing (left).

and the photographer Jean Lartigue, he set off in the footsteps of Chavannes and completed his archaeological inventory of northern China, in Sichuan and the region of Nanjing. It was during this time, in Shaanxi, that he discovered the mausoleum – mentioned in the *Provincial Annals* – of a general who died in 117 BC, Huo Qubing, who was famous for having repelled the Xiongnu, those nomads who were harassing the frontiers of the Han empire (206 BC–AD 220). However, these preliminary investigations only concerned architectural monuments that were visible on the surface. It took some time and some intermediate stages before modern archaeology truly existed in China, a period during which other field workers had to pave the way for archaeologists.

The great expeditions to Central Asia

On the edges of the empire, in eastern Turkestan, Tibet and Mongolia, the adventure had already begun, and continued until the Second World War. The first missions, mostly linked to the political and strategic aims of the British and Russians, were not archaeological. Made up of geographers, geologists, topographers and specialists in natural history, they were concerned with gathering first-hand information to make atlases.

However, the unexpected discovery in 1889 of a Buddhist manuscript, bought at Khotan by a British captain, took Russians, British, Germans, Swedes, Japanese and French – explorers, adventurers or true archaeologists – into the sands of the Taklamakan desert, where they hoped to find traces of the ancient religion. It was their work that led to studies of the Silk Road and Buddhism, as well as of Inner Asia and the Steppes. The Swede Sven Hedin was one of the pioneers of this research that resulted in the discovery of such important sites as Niya and Loulan in Xinjiang (Chinese Turkestan) or Dunhuang in Gansu.

In the course of his expedition of 1899–1902 to eastern Turkestan, Sven Hedin undertook 'a raft voyage across the desert' and produced the first complete map of the Tarim River. Of his barge (below) he said: 'This was to be my observation post, my study and my bedroom. Seated at a work table, I would see the irregularities of the terrain unfold before my eyes, and would immediately put them down on paper, thus producing the map as we progressed.'

The British archaeologist Aurel Stein (centre) was the first person to have access to the walled-up cave of Dunhuang, discovered by a monk in 1900; since then its fabulous contents had been admired by researchers: 'Piled up in several layers…these enormous packets of manuscripts…rose to a height of three metres…. It would have taken a team of learned scribes to take correct care of such an avalanche of texts.' Paul Pelliot, a brilliant French Sinologist (below), buckled down to this task. The study of these paintings and these texts written in Chinese, Tibetan, Khotanese, Sogdian and Ouigour still continues today.

Through the work of Sinologists such as Chavannes, who studied the Chinese documents unearthed by the British explorer and Orientalist Aurel Stein (1862–1943), or his pupil the French translator and Orientalist Paul Pelliot (1878–1945), who, in 1906, himself amassed a wealth of manuscripts, this archaeology of the periphery also had an influence on the archaeology that arose in China.

From 1916 onwards, expeditions to Central Asia stopped for a while, because of the first hostile reactions of the Chinese government. China was preparing to turn one of the most important pages in its archaeological history.

A meeting of the Geological Survey of China in 1936 at the house of Dr Amadeus Grabau, an American geologist (below). The French palaeontologist Teilhard de Chardin remarked to Claude Aragondès on 20 February 1927: 'I have often sung you the praises of the cordiality of these Pekinese meetings of about ten friends, almost close

The creation of the Geological Survey of China

Yet the introduction of western methods, at a time when foreign powers were casting a covetous eye on a humiliated China, did not come about painlessly. It was actually very traumatic. In 1911, at the beginning of the Republic, Beijing, which had become the city of new ideas, was host to numerous scholars. Attitudes changed slowly. Created in 1916 to train the field workers, of which there was a terrible lack in the country, the

friends. Four Chinese...several Americans...two Swedes, Andersson, Sven Hedin, and myself....We experienced the triumph of meeting together, beyond all national and racial barriers.'

Geological Survey of China was very well run by Ding Wenjiang, a Chinese man educated in England. It established a fruitful collaboration with the best foreign specialists, including the Frenchman Pierre Teilhard de Chardin and the Swede Johan Gunnar Andersson, who both had a profound influence on the prehistory and archaeology that emerged in China.

A report by Andersson (below) bears witness to the early period when archaeology, prehistory, geology and palaeontology were still ploughing the same

Andersson: a geologist turned archaeologist

It was Andersson (1874–1960), former director of the Geological Survey of Sweden, who introduced modern archaeology to China.

MEMOIRS

OF

THE GEOLOGICAL SURVEY OF CHINA

PRELIMINARY REPORT

ON

ARCHÆOLOGICAL RESEARCH IN KANSU

BY

J. G. ANDERSSON.

Yet archaeology was not his initial vocation. Andersson arrived in Beijing in 1914 to take up his post as adviser on mining to the Geological Survey of China. He stayed there for ten years.

Andersson took the first step along the road to becoming an archaeologist when he put a plan to his Chinese colleagues to collect mammal fossils and to form reference collections that could be shared between various institutions in China and Sweden. He could not have imagined that the agreement signed between the two countries in 1917 would soon transform his career.

By the end of 1918 numerous fossils had been unearthed, especially in the province of Henan where the search was concentrated.

furrow: 'I was entirely untrained for archaeological research and unprepared to meet the new situation.… The discovery [in autumn 1923] of the rich, and in many respects unique, site at Chu Chia Chai [Zhujiazhai] in the Hsi Ning [Xining] valley marks a turning point in my life.… It determined me to remain in Kansu [Gansu] for one more summer, and it was the beginning of a series of great archaeological discoveries which caused me entirely to abandon my geological work in order to devote the rest of my life to archaeological research.'

Close to Anyang, a discovery had just been made of the first deposits containing inscribed divinatory bones, the famous 'dragon bones', which had until then been sold by private 'excavators' to antiquaries. They were turned into powder and were believed to have healing properties for wounds.

The discovery of Yangshao pots in 1921 marks a turning point

The true turning point took place in 1921 when a prospector brought back some unique samples from Henan that immediately caught Andersson's attention. In April 1921 he went there himself, near the village of Yangshao, where he found a heap of painted pots; but he did not yet know that he had just discovered China's first prehistoric site.

He at once lodged an application for permission to excavate, which constituted the birth of field archaeology in China. Work began in the autumn, in collaboration with P. L. Yuan, of the Geological Survey, and Otto Zdansky, a Viennese palaeontologist. From this time on Andersson's interest and energy were increasingly absorbed by archaeology.

After Yangshao, many discoveries followed. Andersson soon abandoned Henan for Gansu, Qinghai, Mongolia and Tibet; between 1923 and 1924 he led a half-geological and half-archaeological expedition to north-west China. His work brought remarkable rewards: in two years, Andersson discovered more than fifty pre- and proto-historic sites and necropolises. Some of them gave their names to different cultures, and became reference points that are still valid today.

It was some time before Andersson realized the importance of his discoveries. Only when he was consulting, by chance in a Beijing library, the report on the excavation of Anau in Russian Turkestan did he notice the similarity between the painted pots of Yangshao and those unearthed since 1904 by the American expedition of R. Pumpelly. He had just provided the first evidence for the existence in the Far East, like in the eastern Mediterranean, in Mesopotamia or in Persia, of prehistoric painted ceramics. These remains (left, pots of the 3rd millennium BC) enabled Andersson to put forward the first chronological sequence for Chinese protohistory, which he tried to link to that of the Near East. Authorized to take most of the material unearthed during his excavations to Sweden, Andersson later returned half of it to China after his studies, in accordance with the agreement. A museum was built in Stockholm to house his collections.

'Peking Man'

Andersson was also responsible for the discovery in 1922 of China's most famous Palaeolithic site at Zhoukoudian, where so-called 'Peking Man' was found, which marked the development of prehistoric studies in China. The excavation was entrusted to other members of the Geological Survey, such as Pei Wenzhong and Teilhard de Chardin, who became famous for his work there, though he was already known for his palaeontological expeditions to northern China and Mongolia.

Pei, who had returned from France with a solid training in Palaeolithic studies, became – until the early 1980s – one of the men who made the greatest

Teilhard de Chardin (third from right) with his colleagues on the scientific team of Zhoukoudian in 1929: Pei Wenzhong, Yang Zhongjian and two students on his right, and the Canadian anatomist Dr Davidson Black and the American geologist G. B. Barbour on his left. Since 1926 it has been obligatory for foreigners to carry out research and excavations with Chinese colleagues.

THE SKULL OF SINANTHROPUS PEKINENSIS;
A COMPARATIVE STUDY ON A PRIMITIVE HOMINID SKULL

contribution to the development of Chinese archaeology.

After Andersson's departure in 1925, it was necessary to convince a traditionalist community of learned people who considered manual activity to be unworthy of a scholar that the new field methods were useful for studies of antiquity. This task fell to the young patriotic Chinese who were trained in the field by Andersson and his western colleagues on the Geological Survey.

'Making the intruder Chinese…'

The first task of these mediators between the West and China consisted – to coin a phrase from the most famous of them, Li Chi (1896–1979) – of transplanting the ideas of western science on to Chinese soil, of gradually adapting

them to the psychological climate in which they had to be nurtured. In a word, it was a question of 'making the intruder Chinese'. In order to succeed, it was necessary to provide an appropriate institutional framework, to create a new body of researchers 'who could be taught to forget their old ways of thinking'. No doubt none of this would have been possible if China had not been prepared for this small revolution by the atmosphere of intellectual and social change that prevailed at the end of the 1920s. Nor would anything have been

The scientific work undertaken at Zhoukoudian and in the Beijing laboratories by the international team of the Geological Survey acted as a tremendous stimulus to young Chinese researchers at the time. The discovery of the first skull of *Homo pekinensis* on 2 December 1929 was made by Pei and Yang. Numerous excavations have since been carried out at this Lower Palaeolithic site, whose different layers cover a period of about 300,000 years (above, stratigraphic section).

possible without a site where tradition and modernity could meet. Anyang was the scene of this reconciliation between literary learning and field archaeology.

1928: the creation of the Academia Sinica

Chinese historians, who had been influenced since the beginning of the 20th century by western historiography, began to seek empirical proof of the existence of the legendary phases of Chinese history. In this context, the oracular inscriptions engraved on the 'dragon bones' discovered at Anyang opened up new horizons for these scholars. The prospect of increasing the corpus of the oldest Chinese written documents by new discoveries *in situ* meant that field archaeology was taken more seriously. It was put to the test when the first large-scale national excavation was started at Anyang.

This enterprise was granted all the means necessary for success. In 1928 the Nationalist government of Jiang Jieshi settled in Nanjing. The Academia Sinica was especially formed to take charge of the excavation at Anyang and, with it, the Institute of History and Philology, which, thanks to the talents of its director, Fu Sinian, became the principal instrument of archaeological research in China until 1949

Evidence of the divination sessions held by the Shang sovereigns (c. 1300 BC) to make contact with their ancestors, the turtle plastrons (above) found at the site of Anyang (top) are veritable archives of oracular inscriptions.

Anyang or the time of the pioneers

Yet it took eight years and thirteen excavations for the archaeologists' efforts to be rewarded. On 12 June 1936, near the village of Xiaotun, they discovered storage pit no. 127 and its deposit of archives, comprising thousands of fragments of inscribed turtle plastrons. The Shang dynasty (c. 1600–1050 BC), which had been thought to be legendary, without any historical basis, now became reality. Both historians and archaeologists could be well satisfied, because they had discovered at Anyang not only texts but also, and more importantly, a Bronze Age culture that had attained a very advanced stage of development, whose origins and links with the Neolithic sites unearthed in the region by Andersson needed to be investigated.

While the excavations at Anyang were continuing, the road-building work that had been undertaken throughout the country in a surge of modernization was making hitherto unknown parts of the ancient Chinese civilization spring out of the ground. Among the discoveries were bricks with stamped decoration that had formed the inner walls of ancient tombs during the Han period and also numerous funerary figures. These finds later found their way to antiquities dealers or into western museums.

Apart from Anyang, the focus of archaeologists' interest after Andersson continued to be Neolithic sites. In Shandong, in eastern China, Li Chi discovered, at Chengziyai, a new archaeological culture, known as Longshan. Gradually a link was established between the

The director of the Anyang excavations, Li Chi (below right, with Fu Sinian), who was trained by Andersson, was the first Chinese researcher to excavate an archaeological site. He wrote: 'Old China, for centuries a hunting spot for European imperialism, was forced to open her door widely for

whatever the "superior white power" liked to do, including field work in science.' As a student at Harvard, he saw both points of view and was able to combine traditional Chinese methods with the new discipline of archaeology.

oldest vestiges of written history and the newly
discovered prehistoric cultures.

The Sino-Japanese war halts research

During the summer of 1937 war broke out as the
Japanese invaded north-east China. The country was
plunged into a long period of uncertainty, interrupting
the progress of this novice archaeology, which lay

dormant until the foundation of the Republic of China
in 1949. Institutes, libraries and collections left Beijing.
   The Japanese, who had explored Manchuria at the
end of the 19th century, discovered near Dalian the first
prehistoric and Han sites of the region. However, their
work only had a small influence on archaeology in
China. When the Sino-Japanese war ended in 1945,
Li Chi returned to Nanjing and found himself in
charge, helped by young researchers, who later
became the leading lights in Chinese archaeology.

Taiwan or the Republic of China, a new starting point

Yet for Li Chi and a large number of his colleagues in
the Academia Sinica, the resumption in 1947 of the civil
war in northern China between the Nationalists and the
Communists was a prelude to exile in Taiwan, where the
treasures of Anyang later followed them.

毛主席语录

Accompanying the government of Jiang Jieshi and the imperial collections, they arrived in Taiwan during the winter of 1948–9. Far from Henan, which had made him the father of Chinese archaeology, Li Chi continued to play an extremely important role within the still-existing Academia Sinica. Pursuing his research on Anyang, while also developing the archaeology of the island, he trained a new generation of archaeologists at Taipei.

The National Palace Museum in Taipei (opposite) houses the ancient imperial collections, the symbols of the legitimacy of power. Below centre: Guo Muruo, president of the National Academy of Sciences.

A pupil of Li Chi, Xia Nai (1910–85, above), who had a degree in Egyptology from England, was director of the Institute of Archaeology and vice-president of the Academy of Social Sciences. He was the head of Chinese archaeology for more than thirty years. His death in 1985 brought to an end the era in which Chinese archaeology was dominated by scholars trained in the West.

The Marxist vision

On the continent, excavations began again in 1949. However, it was soon apparent that there was a void left by the departure of the Anyang group to Taiwan. Those of Li Chi's colleagues or pupils who had chosen to remain on the continent had to start training new specialists as rapidly as possible. In 1950 a new National Academy of Sciences, conceived on the Soviet model, was created, and took over from the Academia Sinica that had emigrated to Taiwan. Its president, Guo Muruo (1892–1978), who was also vice-president of the National Assembly, was a famous epigrapher. A specialist in archaic bronzes, he had become well known in 1930 for proposing a new approach to studying and interpreting history, scientific materialism. Later he came to personify a period in which archaeology became a state enterprise and Marxism its guiding principle.

This ideological approach was linked with the period when China turned in on itself. For over forty years, from 1949 to 1990, foreigners were viewed as predators and were banned from Chinese archaeological field work; there was no longer any cooperation with the West, and young Chinese people were prevented from studying abroad. From now on the break with the West was complete.

Nevertheless, Chinese archaeology still continued to develop, thanks to the numerous field operations, the

The spectacular discoveries of the 1970s stimulated the development of tourism. Some sites were turned into museums and attract millions of visitors. The city of Xi'an, the country's cultural showcase, has become an obligatory stop in any trip to China (below, an entrance ticket to the museum). Its terracotta soldiers or copies of them travel around the whole world.

training of local archaeologists and the creation of numerous museums and organizations for the protection of the heritage in the provinces. All over the country the excavations led to important discoveries that would gradually make it possible to trace the links between the different sites and cultures, to fit together the pieces of a puzzle that still had many gaps. However, the China of the 1950s was wary of the diversity of its past, and was quick in concealing some of its cultural connections.

The great question remains that of origins

This search for identity was often biased by ideology which, for a long time, affected chronology or cultural attributions. The ideal China, incarnation of a civilized world, was all One. The central plain, irrigated by the valley of the Yellow River, gradually bringing culture to

Opposite: it is also to Xi'an that foreign heads of state are taken. President Clinton made it his first stop – before Beijing during his visit to China in the summer of 1998.

a barbarian periphery, was its ancient heart, and Anyang, where excavations now resumed, its symbol.

From the mid 1960s onwards, the Cultural Revolution put archaeology into another dormant period, despite a few important discoveries. Scientific publications completely ceased until 1971. The great exhibitions exported by China from 1973 onwards were the first step towards its gradual reopening to the outside world. The extraordinary terracotta army of the 3rd century BC, discovered at Xi'an, watching over the eternal rest of its first emperor, soon became the showcase of Chinese archaeology in the West.

Today, China is once again ready to open its doors to a certain extent: since 1991, the law of 1950 forbidding all Chinese-foreign cooperation in archaeological field work has finally been repealed. Excavations now stretch over an immense territory, well beyond the central plain. Regional studies have developed, and research extended to regions and populations that had hitherto been considered marginal. Remains have been discovered there that are even older than those of the 'centre'.

The ideal image of a Chinese civilization that came out of a primordial core has crumbled in the face of these discoveries.

In recent times, large exhibitions have begun to be held in Beijing (left, an entrance ticket to an exhibition at the Imperial Palace Museum). At the same time, through objects displayed abroad, China is gradually trying to establish a new image for itself. Paradoxically, it is the development of the country and its unbridled urbanization that, along with looting, today constitute a threat to its archaeological heritage.

The Neolithic, which is central to the questions about the origin of Chinese civilization, is probably one of the fields in which there has been the most progress since 1949. Thousands of sites, revealing several centres of civilization in the north and south of the country, have been added to the first discoveries and are gradually establishing the image of a plural China.

CHAPTER 2

THE CHINESE NEOLITHIC: FROM SINGULAR TO PLURAL

Figurative depictions are fairly common in the Neolithic Yangshao culture. These pieces come from Shaanxi. Opposite: a bottle with a neck in the form of a human head (the spout is placed at the back). Right: an object in the form of an owl head (c. 4000–3000 BC).

Yangshao: a multi-faceted development

As more discoveries have been made, archaeologists have been able to be more specific about the extraordinary extent of the Yangshao culture, which was first identified by Andersson and is now considered to be one of the major cultures of the Chinese Neolithic (c. 4500–2500 BC). For Yangshao was not just the first Neolithic site discovered in China, nor a simple culture, it is a collection of sites – more than a thousand of them – belonging to different regional facies throughout the middle valley of the Yellow River. From Liaoning to Gansu, they share the same kind of economy and those painted pots that so struck Andersson, though today it is clear that they are very diverse.

The layout of a Neolithic village

Between 1954 and 1957, near Xi'an in Shaanxi, Chinese archaeologists obtained the first precise data on the layout of a Neolithic village at Banpo, which dates back to the early Yangshao (c. 4800–3600 BC). It housed a small agricultural community, and the site – now turned into a museum – was surrounded by a circular ditch and arranged in concentric zones. It underwent several

Below: reconstruction of the village of Banpo: semi-subterranean dwellings, round or square, and storage pits, distributed around a vast central house, have been excavated there. The inhabitants lived from fishing, millet cultivation and breeding dogs and pigs.

These figures, a combination of masks and fishes, were the leitmotiv of the Banpo potters (opposite, on a bowl). They are sometimes interpreted as clan emblems.

periods of habitation, but was intermittently developed, in accordance with the slash-and-burn cultivation.

In the 1970s the excavation of later sites revealed how the villages had gradually been expanded. For example at Dahecun, in Henan, the first terraced houses built on the surface were unearthed. They are rectangular, date to the final Yangshao (c. 3000 BC), and co-exist with the ancient kind of semi-subterranean dwelling.

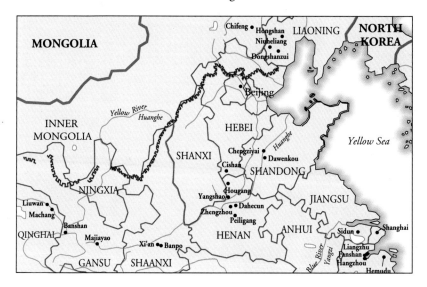

At Banpo, as throughout the Yangshao culture, tombs of children buried in jars have been found close to some houses, but the cemetery, like the potters' kilns, was located outside the village.

The decoration painted on some ceramics was still quite simple. The most original motif, difficult to interpret, comprises a mask combined with fish. This decoration would subsequently undergo considerable development, especially in the north-west.

The above map shows the importance of the great river basins for Neolithic populations. The sites were generally placed on terraces, in the immediate proximity of water sources.

Majiayao or the golden age of painted pottery

The continuation of Andersson's research in Gansu and Qinghai helped bring about a greater understanding of the western extension of Yangshao, of the culture called Majiayao (c. 3500–1500 BC). Archaeologists found vast necropolises and tombs full of painted pots there. On some of them, great circles alternate with anthropomorphic depictions, divinities, shamans or tribal chiefs, the meaning of which is fairly obscure but is probably linked to old agrarian cults. At a time when eastern China was opting for new modes of expression, revealing a more codified spirituality, western China continued for a long time with this tradition of painted pots, which gradually became marginal in the regions that were to develop a Bronze Age of state type. With a different way of life that was more pastoral than agricultural, the north-west progressively moved closer to the stockrearing societies, which became nomadic and played a fundamental role on the margins of China.

The cemetery of Liuwan, in Qinghai, which has 1500 tombs, is one of the largest of the Majiayao culture. In tomb 901 (below), the deceased woman was buried in a wooden coffin, with a pot between her legs and three others by her head. Some large jars were placed outside. The decoration of the early period (below left and right) used a spiral

theme in contrast to the later jars (below centre). In this example four anthropomorphic motifs, head up and head down, alternate on the bulge of the vessel.

At Niuheliang in Liaoning, remains of a structure of unfired brick were discovered and identified as a temple, decorated with female figures modelled in clay – a previously unknown theme. The great earthen face with inlaid eyes (left) represents, according to some archaeologists, the female divinity to which the building was dedicated.

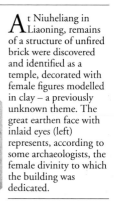

An ancient civilization of jade in the north-east

A few chance finds of jade in the north-east put researchers on to the trail of an original culture that existed in Inner Mongolia and Liaoning between 3800 and 2700 BC. They gave it the name of Hongshan, a site excavated by the Japanese in 1938, whose full importance had not been realized at that time. These jades, which continue a tradition begun in the same region around 5000 BC, came from cist graves, and indeed often constituted their only grave goods. Most of them are pendants, of various forms – 'hooked clouds', tortoises or birds with spread wings, perforated disks, 'pig-dragons', or 'horse-hoof shaped' objects – and were probably attached to the body or clothes of the deceased.

The jade 'pig-dragon' (above) owes its name to its rolled-up body and its squashed snout. Placed on the chest of the dead, these perforated figurines with large eyes characterize the Hongshan culture (c. 3500 BC). They seem to have had a symbolic or ritual significance for the people of the time.

At Pingliangtai, in Henan (left), the remains of a tamped-earth enclosure of about 185 square metres (1990 square feet) were excavated in 1979. *Intra muros*, the archaeologists unearthed a section of subterranean drainage, uninscribed divinatory bones and rectangular houses built at ground level or on low platforms.

The tall-stemmed cup (left), like the three-footed jug (below), is characteristic of the Longshan culture in Shandong. Made of wheelthrown black pottery, as thin (sometimes less than a millimetre) as an eggshell, it was probably intended for ceremonial libations.

Their precise function remains unknown. Rather than simple ornaments, they seem to have been related to a fertility cult. At any rate, this is what is suggested by the excavations carried out in 1981 at two other sites, Dongshanzui and Niuheliang in Liaoning. The unique and complex constructions that were discovered there have been interpreted as temples: stone platforms, reinforced with terracotta cylinders, which were associated with small female figurines. In any case, both the symbolic dimension and the particular value of jade in the Chinese civilization – perhaps comparable to the esteem in which gold, silver and precious stones are held by westerners – were already present in the Hongshan period.

Longshan and its developments

Also in northern China, but this time from Shandong to Shaanxi, archaeologists have discovered hundreds of sites corresponding to different regional or chronological variations of the

Longshan culture (c. 2500–1700 BC), identified by Andersson in 1928. During this period, this was a prosperous region where elements from the coast met traditions peculiar to the valley of the Yellow River. There was an increasing differentiation in riches, while in Henan the first fortified sites were appearing. Agriculture appears to have been fully developed. Cows, sheep, dogs and pigs were all domesticated. Wheat and barley were cultivated, together with millet.

The toolkit was perfected, especially with shell sickles. Pottery was also undergoing considerable evolution. While the use of the potter's wheel was spreading, handthrown painted pots were in decline, giving way to grey pots with impressed decoration. It was in eastern China that these new trends are most evident, through black, finely polished, wheelthrown pieces known as 'eggshell'. The slenderness and purity of their forms take precedence over colour, which is replaced by a more restrained set of ribs, cutouts or incisions that are also present on jades.

Before Longshan, a culture linking north and south

Thanks to research along the east coast, it has also been possible to bring to light some of the missing links between the Yangshao and the Longshan cultures. As

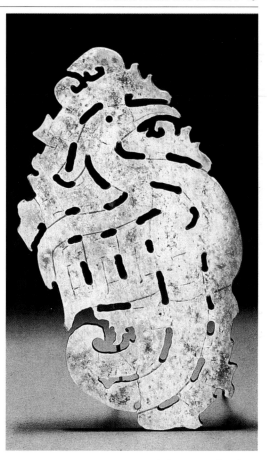

Even more than for its ceramics, the Neolithic of the east coast is renowned for the abundance of its jade objects, which are often of high quality. The long-tailed crested bird, finely engraved on this plaque of white jade, is characteristic of the Longshan culture.

in the central plain, archaeologists in this region have gradually found older and older sites, which they first believed came from northern China.

The Dawenkou culture (c. 4500–2500 BC), identified in 1959 in Shandong, is one of their most important discoveries. Also found in the neighbouring provinces of Anhui, Jiangsu and Henan, it belongs to a group of cultures that seem to have developed quite early in the lower valley of the Yellow River, in the Huai and north of the Blue River. This culture linked the traditions of northern and southern China, and is primarily known from its graves. Some skeletons, as often in the south, display cranial deformations associated with the ritual practice of the extraction of upper incisors. The distribution of grave goods indicates an already hierarchical society. Some rich tombs contain bones of sacrificed pigs. A few jade pieces have also been found, and various precious or exotic objects of turquoise, bone, horn or ivory. The pots are quite elaborate, and include painted vessels that point to contacts with Yangshao, but also tripods and cups with perforated stems that are common in the south, and grey wheelthrown pieces, made of a fine paste, which foreshadow those of Longshan. The bird motif, compared by some to a totem, was recurrent in southern cultures, and is already present here in the form of incised signs.

Northern China before Yangshao, a civilization based on millet

As the different cultures of the Neolithic of northern China were being set in place, one essential question still remained unanswered: what happened before

L eft: a pot from the Dawenkou culture. Its openwork decoration is typical of the cultures of the south-east. Below: a four-footed sandstone grindstone and its roller from the Peiligang culture.

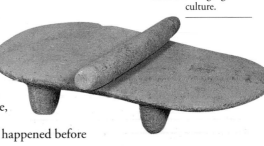

The history of China and its first centres of farming is closely linked to the two great rivers that shaped its landscape. In the north, the Yellow River, or Huanghe (left, in Shanxi province) is filled with alluvia, and its fluctuating course was the cause of many catastrophic floods. In the centre, the Yangzi, or Blue River, constitutes an important communication route. This territory is not only immense, but also features some strong contrasts: between the semi-arid plain of the north, the yellow land of loess and millet, and the green hills of the south, whose humid climate, ideal for rice cultivation, today provides two to three annual harvests; between the east coast, densely populated, and the north or west, regions of mountains, steppes and great deserts; and finally between the fertile interior of China of the sedentary farmers, and peripheral China with its arid confines, a country of stockrearing, of nomads, inhabited by non-Chinese populations.

Yangshao? The problem was only solved quite recently. Research in this field really began after the Cultural Revolution. In 1976 the first excavations started at Cishan in Henan and were soon followed by work at Peiligang in Hebei, the eponymous sites of a culture dating to between 5500 and 4900 BC. Here archaeologists found grains of millet, the oldest known in the valley of the Yellow River, the cradle of this cereal's domestication. Associated with toothed sickles and footed millstones with matching long rollers, these grains came from storage-pits dug around the houses, which were themselves semi-subterranean. The populations who lived in these first villages raised pigs and dogs, a practice that later became characteristic of northern China, as well as chickens, probably the oldest domesticated examples in the world.

Southern China, a different world

This millet-growing China faced the rice-growing China. The exploration of the southern regions, which began in 1930, 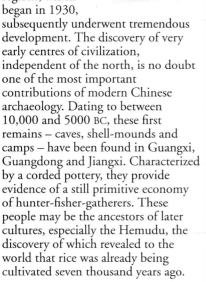 subsequently underwent tremendous development. The discovery of very early centres of civilization, independent of the north, is no doubt one of the most important contributions of modern Chinese archaeology. Dating to between 10,000 and 5000 BC, these first remains – caves, shell-mounds and camps – have been found in Guangxi, Guangdong and Jiangxi. Characterized by a corded pottery, they provide evidence of a still primitive economy of hunter-fisher-gatherers. These people may be the ancestors of later cultures, especially the Hemudu, the discovery of which revealed to the world that rice was already being cultivated seven thousand years ago.

The middle Blue River, cradle of rice domestication

The site of Hemudu, excavated until 1978, was discovered in 1973 in Zhejiang. Dating to about 5000–4770 BC, it is the oldest Neolithic site in the region of Hangzhou Bay. Archaeologists discovered the remains of a lakeshore habitation built of wood on piles – a type of construction that was hitherto totally unknown here, and very different from the earthen houses of northern China. The people

who lived here were probably linked with early populations of the Pacific Islands.

Yet the site's originality lies not only in its dwellings but also in all of its remains and reveals a fully-fledged civilization. The economy was based not on millet, as in the north, but on rice. The rice grains found on the site were cultivated in flooded fields with hoes made of animal shoulder-blades.

Left: landscape of rice fields in the province of Guizhou. The flooded terraced fields are given over to intensive agriculture.

At the site of Hemudu in Zhejiang (stamp, opposite) objects of ivory and wood have been found and pots

This discovery called into question the idea that culture had spread from the north and that Chinese rice originated from India. It made it possible to locate the oldest known centre of rice domestication in the basin of the Blue River. Remains even older than those found at Hemudu were recently discovered at Pengtoushan in Hunan. They could push the origin of this cereal back to around 6000 BC.

with an incised decoration of birds, plants and pigs (above). Beside bones of pig, dog and buffalo, which were domesticated, there were also monkeys, sheep, cervids, rhinoceros, elephants, tigers and bears, as well as various fish, reptiles and tortoises.

Art, ritual and power in the final Neolithic, the splendour of Liangzhu

In the final Neolithic, the Liangzhu culture (c. 3000–2000 BC), found in

Zhejiang, Jiangsu and the Shanghai region, is as important as the Hemudu. First discovered in 1936, it represents, more than any other culture, the dynamism of China's coastal regions in a period when a gap was widening between the more conservative western regions and those of the more innovatory east. Liangzhu thus shares with the Longshan of Shandong elegant wheelthrown black ceramics of fine paste, a taste for a decoration of perforated cutouts or engravings, and stemmed forms.

However, even more than Longshan or Hongshan, Liangzhu is renowned for its jade-working, which reached great heights. It was a codified art through which the nobility of the material, the perfection of the manufacture and the complexity of the decoration became the emblems of an elite and a particular ideology. A deceased person's status was often measured by the jades preserved in their tomb.

One of the richest, tomb no. 3 of Sidun in Jiangsu, contained more than two hundred, which literally covered the deceased's body: ritual weapons and, especially, long cubic cylinders, known as *cong*, associated with *bi* disks, round jades with a hole in the centre. Usually placed on the stomach of the dead, these objects have a ritual or symbolic meaning. The way in which they are decorated is also symbolic:

Tomb no. 3 at Sidun (below) belongs to a man of about twenty, probably of high rank. Traces were found here of a cremation ritual. After placing most of the jades in the pit, a fire was lit, on to which the body and other jades were added.

The two *cong*, ritual cylinders of white jade (below), come from tomb no. 12 at Fanshan (Zhejiang). Of exceptional quality, they are engraved with a composite divinity (detail left), made up of a feathered creature clutching in front of it an animal mask with large protruding eyes. This motif constitutes the main, almost exclusive decoration of the Liangzhu jades. It mostly appears in a simplified form (on the corners). The motif is then limited to the superimposition of the human and animal figures, reduced to their essential traits. These depictions could be the origin of the decoration of the Bronze Age masks.

they depict an anthropomorphic divinity, with feathers for hair, associated with an animal face that exists in several variations. The elliptical version of this theme brings out the features that constitute the essence of the motif and are sufficient to evoke the whole thing: the eyes, mouth and hairstyle. The bird motif that is sometimes associated with these figures has the same emblematic meaning. This decoration forms a link with the Bronze Age, when the relationship between art, politics and religion, already so perceptible at Liangzhu, was established for centuries.

The appearance of writing, metallurgy, the first cities and the birth of a centralized power mark the transition from the Neolithic to the Bronze Age. In China, this phase of profound change occurred between about 2000 and 1600 BC.

CHAPTER 3

THE SHANG: THE EMERGENCE OF A CIVILIZATION

The motif of a tiger devouring a human (right) is common on Shang bronzes. It has been interpreted in a variety of ways: as a representative of authority or protection, presentation of the shaman and his helper. In contrast, the monumental bronze statuary found at Sanxingdui in Sichuan (opposite) remains exceptional.

Anyang, the original cradle?

Three royal dynasties – those of the Xia (c. 2000–
1600 BC), Shang (c. 1600–1050 BC) and Zhou
(c. 1050–221 BC) – mark the end of prehistory and the
start of civilization in China, according to the texts that
ignore their neighbours. The Bronze Age traditionally
amounts to the royal dynasties from the valley of the
Yellow River, the embodiment of the civilized world.

From 1928 onwards, the symbolic importance of the
excavations at Anyang, in the heart of this region, only
served to reinforce this idealized view of the original
cradle. For years, all that was known of the Shang,
until then considered to be legendary, was this site, the
remains of their last capital, which had been occupied
from about 1300 to 1050 BC.

Anyang provided dazzling evidence for a mature
Bronze Age, and became the symbol of China's past
values, of what was most recognizably Chinese about it;
yet it left one essential question unanswered – from
where did this sophisticated metallurgy originate? The
hypothesis, put forward by Li Chi, of influences from

Above: the excavation
of the royal
necropolis of Anyang
in the 1930s. Inclined
ramps provided access
to the pit (in the
foreground).

western Asia, was rejected by his successors, who were anxious to restore national honour. The question has still not been completely solved today. After the departure of the old members of the Academia Sinica to Taiwan, many years were devoted to research into the previous history of this 'golden age', and especially into the ancient capitals, which historical chronicles located in Henan.

First cities, first bronzes

Moreover, it was in this region that the first missing links were found between the Neolithic and the Bronze Age of Anyang. In the early 1950s a collection of remains stretching for dozens of kilometres, and including several occupation layers, was first discovered near Zhengzhou. On the hill of Erligang, the ruins of an imposing tamped-earth rampart 7 kilometres (over 4 miles) long was uncovered. It was a city that was probably the capital of the Shang between 1500 and 1400 BC, before they settled at Anyang.

From 1958 onwards, and then again in 1983, even older remains, thought to belong to the direct ancestors of those from Erligang, were unearthed at Erlitou: another fortified city, and the remains of a palace occupied during the first half of the 2nd millennium, between 1700 and 1500 BC. These finds provided conclusive evidence of the first Shang and their predecessors, which some assumed to be the Xia, a still mythical dynasty whose founder, Yu the Great, tamer of the waters, supposedly invented metallurgy.

A clearer picture of the link between these first cities and the fortified villages of the final Neolithic was

The *yue*, or ceremonial axes (below), were used for human or animal sacrifice.

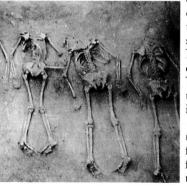

Tomb M1001 of Houjiazhuang at Anyang is the largest of the eleven great cruciform tombs of the Shang royal necropolis. Numerous sacrificial victims, perhaps prisoners, were unearthed here in small pits or near the tomb's access ramps. Decapitated torsos (left) and skulls were buried separately. Sacrificed humans were also found beneath the foundations of the important buildings in the capital.

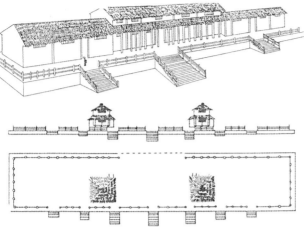

Right: reconstruction of a double-roofed building, a temple or palace, at Anyang. Left: two pavilions with an upper floor, on a platform of tamped earth, also at Anyang.

formed later on. Immediately emphasis was placed on the extraordinary continuity of a civilization that, at the beginning of the 2nd millennium BC, already carried the seeds of the future Forbidden City. Like its remote descendant, the Shang city comprises two poles. Always in the centre, the palaces and the temple dedicated to the ancestors of the royal lineage, surrounded by colonnades, are recognizable by the vast tamped-earth terraces that were their foundations. This political and administrative heart of the city was reserved for the king, the priests and the aristocracy. A real 'palace-city', it was a closed and hierarchical place, protected by an enclosure. Villages, markets, artisans' quarters and necropolises were kept outside the walls.

This bronze plaque inlaid with turquoise (left) was found in 1981 in tomb no. 4 at Erlitou, but its function is unknown. Placed on the chest of the deceased, it has four rings and is decorated on one side with a monster face with protruding eyes. It was found with lacquerware and a little bronze bell.

The *jue*, or tripod cups (opposite), were used for warming cereal wine. This one comes from the site of Erlitou. It is small (22.5 cm or 8¾"), still quite irregularly manufactured and undecorated. It was made of an alloy of copper and tin.

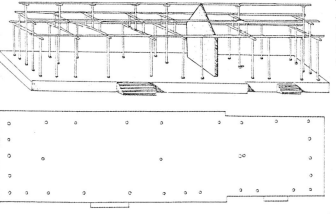

Bronze was a symbol of royal authority, reserved for the manufacture of weapons, pieces of chariots or harnesses, and ritual vessels; it belonged to the realm of the sacred and, for the Shang, represented two functions that were essential to the state: war and sacrifices. Thus bronze receptacles were an integral part of the sovereign's cult of worship in memory of his ancestors. As instruments of communication with the dead, they were used to present offerings of wine, meat and cereals during ritual banquets accompanied by music. Preceded by sessions of divination, the ceremonies were

often associated with sacrifices of livestock. The offerings table (following page) and its twelve wine vessels were discovered in 1901 at Baoji in Shaanxi.

Erlitou, the missing link

The study of the kilns, potters' workshops and the foundries filled with terracotta moulds and models have enabled researchers to establish the link between ceramic and bronze technology. The first evidence of the use of metal at the end of the Neolithic confirms that production was on a small scale and only small objects were involved. It was at Erlitou that, in 1973, the first bronze vessels were found, dating to about 1600 BC: four *jue*, tripod cups with angular shapes and thin, bare walls. Despite their slightly crude appearance, these small vessels display all the distinctive characteristics of Chinese metallurgy, especially the technique of upside-down casting in segmented clay moulds. Their shape foreshadows the later developments of a highly specialized

and codified art that, through bronze, provided a restricted elite with a privileged means of expression. It lasted for almost a thousand years.

From Erligang to Anyang, the development of a technical and artistic tradition

The bronze technology at Erligang was more diversified than at Erlitou and produced pieces that were on a par with the remarkable objects from Anyang. The bronzesmiths were now capable of producing vessels of up to a metre (over 3 feet) in height, often cast in two stages. Because of the importance of ritual, new forms of vessel emerged throughout the Shang period – for warming, pouring or drinking alcohol, a kind of beer made from fermented cereals. Decoration was first limited to a horizontal band punctuated with circular motifs that foreshadow the protruding eyes of a *taotie*, an animal mask whose symbolic meaning is largely unknown. It gradually spread and grew richer with a fantastic bestiary dominated by this theme of the mask, which became the leitmotiv of Anyang's art. The fabulous creatures were later associated with more

The evolution of Shang decoration (left, the *taotie* mask) is linked to the development of smelting techniques and to the subdivisions of the mould, which give a fixed framework for the different motifs. In the Anyang period (above), the traces of joins of the different parts of the mould had become decorative ridges. Decoration then emerged from the very circumscribed framework of the first decorations of the Erligang phase, represented by the food vessel opposite. It measures 1 metre in height and weighs 86.4 kilos!

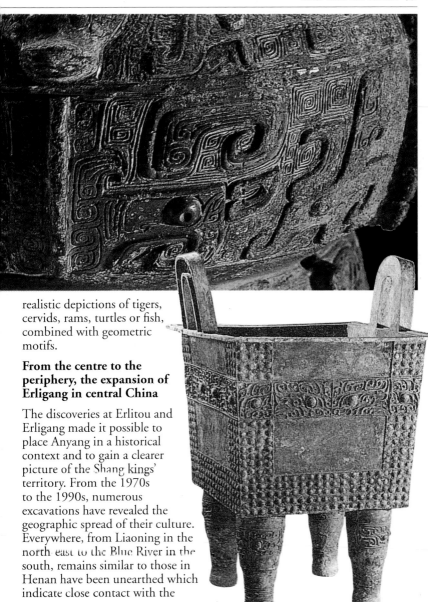

realistic depictions of tigers, cervids, rams, turtles or fish, combined with geometric motifs.

From the centre to the periphery, the expansion of Erligang in central China

The discoveries at Erlitou and Erligang made it possible to place Anyang in a historical context and to gain a clearer picture of the Shang kings' territory. From the 1970s to the 1990s, numerous excavations have revealed the geographic spread of their culture. Everywhere, from Liaoning in the north-east to the Blue River in the south, remains similar to those in Henan have been unearthed which indicate close contact with the

metropolis. Excavations outside the basin of the Yellow River produced surprising results for Chinese archaeologists. In these regions they discovered centres of civilization which, though contemporaneous with the Shang, were ignored by the texts and were often profoundly original.

Independent regional centres in southern China

The spread of Erligang culture stimulated relationships between very remote regions and caused regional centres to develop outside the royal domain. Motifs and techniques provide clear evidence of these relationships. They can be traced well beyond the Blue River, and especially in Hunan, where the bronzes of Ningxiang, discovered in the 1960s, reveal the originality of the southern style. This southern tradition is characterized by the production of bells and vessels in the shape of elephants, tigers or buffaloes, sculptures of imposing proportions.

Jiangxi provides another example. Here, in the 1970s, archaeologists were amazed to discover a site from the beginning of the Bronze Age, called Wucheng, and were struck by the high quality of its glazed ceramics.

The appearance of writing dates back to the 2nd millennium BC. Apart from inscriptions on bronze, the oracular inscriptions on cattle shoulder-blades and turtle plastrons (left) constitute the bulk of the corpus that is known at present. Cavities were dug into the reverse side of the bone and, when these were burned, they produced T-shaped cracks on the other side that materialized the word of the royal ancestors. After being read by the king, who alone had the power of interpreting them, various notations were made by specialized scribes. They mention the date, the name of the diviner and the object of divination (most frequently rains and harvests), then two hypotheses, set out in columns (on the right, what the king hoped to see happen, on the left the opposite forecast), and finally the verification of the prediction.

Opposite: a wine vessel (bottom) decorated with four rams in haut-relief, characteristic of the southern style. The one at top left, decorated with anthropomorphic faces, is exceptional.

The tomb of Xin'gan in Jiangxi

It was only in 1989 that excavators really realized the importance of this region when, close to Xin'gan, they unearthed the remains of a tomb that was unique to southern China, although damaged by the waters of the Gan River. Here they again found glazed stoneware, a symbol of high status, and grave goods that make this tomb, dating to the 13th century BC, the second richest from the Shang period: more than 350 ceramics, 150 jades and especially 50 vessels, 4 bells and more than 400 tools and weapons of bronze. When the objects in this tomb were studied more closely, it was noticed that they came from different sources and periods, a phenomenon that was probably quite widespread, though it is not well recognized. Some bronze pieces, similar to Shang vessels, were probably imported from the north and hoarded; others were modified and adapted to local tastes. Most of them reveal the existence of a highly developed regional bronze culture. Cast locally, the pieces differ from the objects of Anyang. The groupings of bronzes themselves seem

Bronze drums (below) are characteristic of south central China, where the first bronze bells seem to have been manufactured.

to obey different rules and correspond to another conception of ritual.

Anyang rediscovered: the tomb of Lady Hao

Knowledge of the royal art of the Shang at Anyang, and in particular of the ritual bronze vessels, was also increased when, in 1976, the tomb of a woman who died around 1200 BC was discovered near Xiaotun.

The tomb of Xin'gan in Jiangxi during excavations (above and opposite top). A bronze standard in the form of a horned face was associated with ritual vessels.

All the characteristic elements of pre-imperial funerary architecture are already present here: an exterior construction intended for funerary rites, a timber lining placed at the bottom of a deep pit, and human and animal sacrifices. For the first time in the history of the Shang, an archaeological discovery could be related to an individual who was known from texts: Fu Hao (Lady Hao), consort of Wu Ding, a ruler of Shang and a great army leader. She was identified from the inscription on bronzes, a practice that became common at the end of the Shang period. This phenomenon added an extra dimension to already highly precious objects.

Her tomb – the only one belonging to a member of the royal family that had not been disturbed – contained the most important and most complete group of bronzes from the Shang dynasty, more than 200 vessels. It reveals the principal attributes of an elite at the height of its prosperity. The rest of the grave goods, which include almost 7000 cowrie shells, 750 jades and 560 stone and bone objects, were also exceptionally rich. Beautiful ritual jade weapons and numerous bronze weapons evoke not only the warlike qualities of the deceased, but also the close link between war and ritual under the Shang.

The kings of Anyang and their neighbours: Sanxingdui

Nevertheless, the magnificent works of the sovereigns of Anyang were not unique. A discovery made in July 1986 by archaeologists, probably one of the most important of the century, revealed that other regions, like the Sichuan basin, also developed an original and

The Fu Hao bronzes bear the mark of the elite of her time: large dimensions, a monumental style. They come in many shapes, with complex decoration. There are rare or new forms – the stand with three pots for cooking (opposite), vessels in the form of an owl, a quadruped or a house and exotic pieces, bronzes from the south or daggers from the steppes, which the lady must have collected. The stone kneeling figurine (below) and the drinking cup in elephant ivory inlaid with turquoise (below left) were also part of her funerary goods.

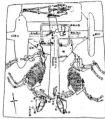

The chariot, probably borrowed by the Shang from their steppe neighbours, was for them a symbol of royal power. The excavations at Anyang yielded several chariots, buried in pits close to important buildings. The chariots were associated with horses (diagram above) and the main weapons of the period, halberds, spears, bows and arrows. This tradition, maintained by their successors, continued for a long time after them (left, a pit of the 5th–3rd century BC).

sophisticated bronze civilization during the period when Anyang began to be occupied. Labourers in a brickworks, who were working at Sanxingdui on the edge of a site known to archaeologists since 1929 and excavated several times, unearthed jade pieces that caught their attention.

More than seven hundred exceptional objects of gold leaf, bronze and jade were discovered next to carbonized animal bones,

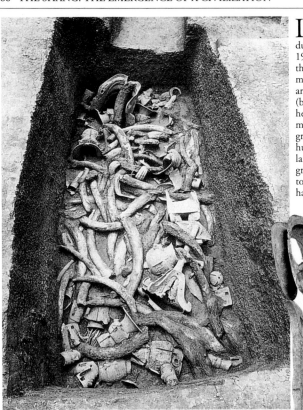

Left: sacrificial pit no. 2 at Sanxingdui, during its discovery in 1986. It contained more than 400 objects. The most astonishing pieces are undoubtedly masks (below) and bronze heads (opposite). The masks, which are more grotesque than the human figures, have large ears and a grimacing mouth. A total of twelve masks have been found. This one, 82.6 cm (32½") tall, has a highly developed large nose. Rectangular perforations on the sides must have allowed them to be fixed to a support.

cowrie shells and elephant tusks. These remains of a sacrifice, during which animals and various offerings had been burnt and ritually buried in two great pits, revolutionized research into the Bronze Age. As in Jiangxi in the Erligang period, some imported and other hybrid objects point to contacts with the Shang, though most of the finds are unique. A tree of spirits or human depictions in bronze reveal an extremely powerful sculptural art, a perfect mastery of casting techniques, and unknown ritual practices. These pits were linked to a fortified site whose remains were found over ten kilometres (six miles).

Despite the distorted image provided by texts, the power of the Shang kings was not universal. They had mighty neighbours with whom they maintained links, some closer than others. It was not those from Sichuan, but others, from closer at hand, who eventually overthrew them.

Forty bronze human heads (below) were found at Sanxingdui, at the edge of the pit. Some of them were filled with cowrie shells or bore traces of polychrome decoration: black on the hair, red on the lips. They provide evidence for ritual practices that were very different from those of the Shang. It is not known whether they were attached to a body and what their function could have been: divinity, shaman, ancestor? In a similar way, the role of the large statue (left) is unknown. This spectacular, monumental person, 1.72 metres (67¾") high, stands on a high pedestal decorated with an upside-down mask. The object he held in his arms, perhaps an elephant tusk, has disappeared.

In the mid-2nd millennium BC, the Zhou – who had hitherto been unobtrusive neighbours of the Shang – took power. An era of profound upheavals had begun. The great social, economic and technological transformations, along with the changes in values and ways of thinking, led China from royalty to empire.

CHAPTER 4

EIGHT CENTURIES OF EVENTFUL HISTORY

At the time when the kingdoms were tearing each other apart, swords (right) were made in large numbers by highly specialized workshops. A new preoccupation with protecting the deceased emerged at the same time. Halberdiers and mythical figures (opposite) were used for this purpose.

The buried treasures of the Zhou

The history of the Zhou goes back to the 13th century BC, but at that time they were just a clan that originated in the north-west of China. From their territory in Shaanxi they gradually spread eastwards and then, claiming to have a mandate from Heaven, they overthrew the Shang and set up their capital near Xi'an. The reign of the Western Zhou began around 1050 BC, centred on Shaanxi. Their new territory was too vast to be governed directly, and was divided into fiefs where vassals were delegated to rule.

When they took power, the Zhou settled in the west of Shang territory, in Shaanxi – hence their name of the Western Zhou. In 771 BC they moved their capital to the east, to Henan, and became known as the Eastern Zhou. Left: map showing sites of the Zhou period.

The ceremonial wine vessel (opposite) dates from the 10th century BC. Its decoration is typical for the period. The *taotie* mask was replaced by large long-tailed birds arranged on either side of the central ridge.

In the region of Qishan and Fufeng, numerous discoveries have revealed traces of the Zhou before they took power. These finds have made it possible to evaluate the differences between them and the Shang, particularly in the field of metallurgy. Most of the bronzes of the Western Zhou come from caches deposited in 771 BC during troubles that forced the sovereigns to leave their capital and that put an end to the dynasty. In 1976 peasants and labourers unearthed these vessels from different periods that had belonged to several generations of one family.

One of the most important treasures (left) is the collection of 103 bronzes unearthed in 1976 in Zhuangbai near Fufeng in Shaanxi. Dating to the 11th–8th centuries BC, they include a plate bearing one of the longest inscriptions known on bronze: 284 characters. The study of these inscriptions, which were very short under the Shang, but which became longer under the Zhou, has enriched the knowledge of the period for historians, epigraphers and archaeologists. They are remarkable family archives that evoke, through a date, a place, the mention of a gift or of an investiture, the status of the owner of the bronzes and the circumstances of their manufacture.

Legacy of the Shang and new motifs

These bronzes cover practically the whole stylistic evolution of the Western Zhou. The oldest specimens, strongly inspired by the bronze tradition of Anyang, reflect the desire of the Zhou to adopt as their own the cultural ideals of the Shang. However, these motifs were soon enriched with new themes, borrowing from the repertoire of western and southern regions their monumentality and exuberance, as well as a taste for haut-reliefs and ridges, and for zoomorphic shapes and decoration. Various vessels, like ritual display units, also correspond to a metallurgical tradition peculiar to the Zhou.

From the 10th century BC onwards, a completely new style emerges. Previously unknown motifs, probably influenced by the south – coiled dragons, humanoid faces, elegant tufted or crested birds with long tails – now contend with the *taotie* mask for pre-eminence. They are found on the jades that appeared frequently in tombs, where various influences, made possible by the Zhou's position between the north-west and south-west, are evident.

The bronze vessel and display unit above and opposite represent a form that was very fashionable under the Zhou. Left: large bells without clappers in a restoration workshop at Fufeng (Shaanxi).

A ritual reform

At the end of the Western Zhou, sets, shapes and decoration of bronzes became more stereotyped. They underwent a profound change, a real revolution in terms of ritual. The vessels for alcohol that had been in use since the Shang were abandoned in favour of food vessels, with associated tripods and display units. A special feature of ritual practice was the pealing of bells. Inscriptions became longer, while decoration was more sober, with a trend towards abstraction. Dragons' bodies became a ribbon whose undulations avoided the symmetry of ancient compositions.

The dragon decoration, undulating all round the vessel in a continuous movement, foreshadows the interweaving, curling style that became typical under the Zhou (below, a large ceremonial basin).

Zoomorphic compositions were transformed and lost legibility. Art in jade also underwent profound changes. In the tombs – those of the lords of Jin at Qucun in Shanxi, those of the lords of Guo at Shangcunling in Henan – excavated since 1990, the bodies of the deceased disappear under a heap of jades.

The jade pieces below form a mask. They were found in the tomb of a lord of Guo at Shangcunling in Henan. The painstaking work of the excavators made it possible to restore each piece to its original position.

中國人民郵政

8分

利簋

西周（公元前十一世紀——公元前七七一年）一九七六年陝西臨潼出土。食器。器高二八、口径二二厘米；重七·九五公斤。銘文記載了武王灭商的日期。

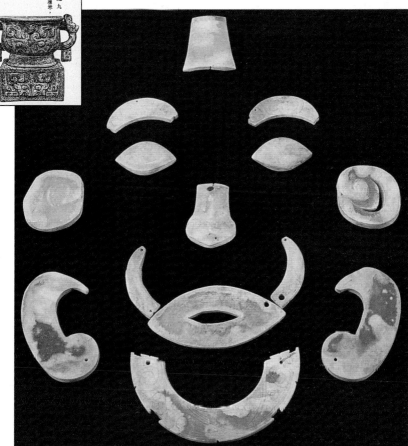

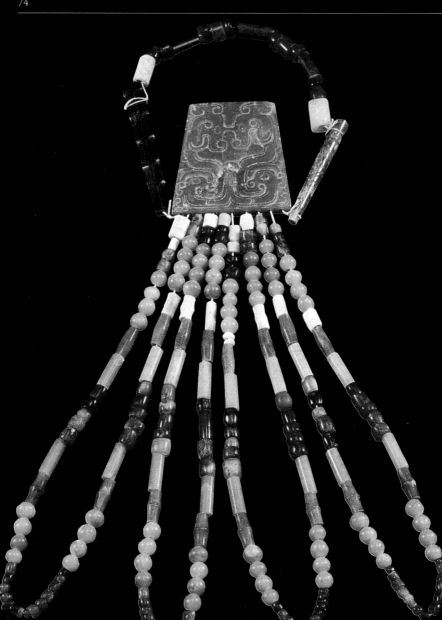

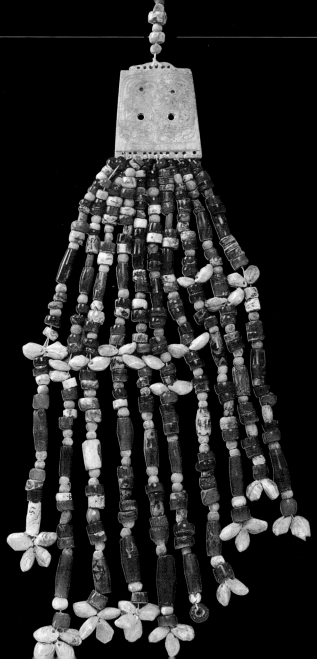

At the end of the Western Zhou and the start of the Eastern Zhou, the lords of the states of Guo in Henan and of Jin in Shanxi were buried with rich grave goods that reflected, in their extent and composition, the rank of the deceased. Along with ceremonial vessels and peals of bronze bells, jade played a prominent role. It still appeared only in disks, ritual weapons, long necklaces and heavy pendants, or masks composed of perforated pieces of jade sewn on to cloth (previous page), but the idea of enveloping the deceased in jade already existed. Later it underwent considerable changes. The jewellery on the left, made of jade, agate and turquoise, was found in the tomb of a lord of the small state of Ying at Pingdingshan in Henan. The necklace on the right, which includes shells, comes from Tianma-Qucun in Shanxi. Other symbols of high status, such as objects of cast iron, bimetallic tools or weapons (iron and bronze), were innovations of this period and also appear in the tombs.

The Eastern Zhou: the beginning of chaos

In 771 BC the transfer of the capital to Henan marked not only the start of a new reign, that of the Eastern Zhou (770–221 BC), but also the end of an era. The relative stability of the preceding centuries was followed by a long period of chaos, marked by the conflicts between the feudal lords who had enlarged their domains and now tried to supplant the reigning dynasty. This first phase, characterized by a reinforcement of regional identities, corresponds to the period known as 'Spring and Autumn Annals' (770–475 BC). The weakening of the Zhou's central power gave the principalities that had emerged from the former fiefs the chance for liberation, a time of the 'Warring States' (475–221 BC). The large kingdoms absorbed the small, competing with each other in wealth, whereas the ancient rites gradually lost their significance. Each

The princes possessed powerful armies and engaged in merciless wars, using thousands of foot soldiers, helped by units of cavalry, on the battlefield. The sword was borrowed from the nomadic populations present

to the west and on the northern frontier. Left: the sword of King Goujian of Yue, who reigned from 496 to 465 BC.

The terracotta mould (left) of a person with raised arms forms the stand of a bronze tray. It comes from the foundry of Houma. Despite the wars, agriculture was booming, thanks to the invention of the plough and a new toolkit in cast iron, a technique that was not used in the West before the end of the Middle Ages.

court had its own fortified city, its coinage, its workshops and its artists. This rivalry encouraged the development of trade between regions and the emergence of a philosophical thought personified by Confucius (551–479 BC).

The proliferation of cultures is echoed in the profusion of archaeological discoveries: thousands of tombs and only a few capitals. At the start of the dynasty, the Eastern Zhou continued the traditions that were begun by their predecessors. The decorative formulas that now appeared remained in force for several centuries. The dominant style was characterized by interlocking movement. In the 6th and 5th centuries BC, regional differences gradually became grouped around two great traditions, the states of Jin in the north and Chu in the south.

The Jin tradition in the north

The first research on the tradition of Jin dates back to 1956 when, at Houma in Shanxi, the remains of a city, its capital between 584 and 450 BC, were found. At an enormous bronze foundry, archaeologists unearthed more than 30,000 fragments of moulds corresponding to different styles, which pointed to a highly specialized art and to technical innovations that permitted the mass-production of repetitive motifs from small dies.

This discovery also made it possible to attribute to the Jin the very special production of bronzes called Liyu, a name taken from the small village in Shanxi where a peasant discovered them in 1923. Today the term designates a decorative style that corresponds to the appearance in China of the oldest figurative scenes.

These vessels, characteristic Jin products, were made in the foundry of Houma (centre, fantastic creatures, the decoration of an inlaid bronze vessel; below, a vessel from Liyu). The abstract interlace decoration contrasts with the naturalism of the small animals made in high relief.

Inlays and figurative scenes: a link with the nomadic world?

The reappearance in the 6th century BC of the technique of inlay, reserved by the Shang for the decoration of their ceremonial weapons, is probably linked to the strengthening of ties with the nomadic world of Eurasia. This technique can be found on various objects that the Chinese lost no time in borrowing and adapting to their taste, such as buckles. There was also a predilection for contrasts in colour and for narrative scenes. These influences are particularly noticeable on vessels with inlaid decoration portraying ceremonial scenes of the court or hunting, in which the protagonists, cutouts as profile silhouettes, recall the depictions on rocks, or those of the applied felt or gold-leaf so beloved of the steppe populations. Other vessels, decorated with hybrid beings, devote a large amount of space to fantastic images. These figures reflect religious themes that are not peculiar to northern China, where they were abandoned by the mid-5th century BC. They are also found at Chu on lacquerware of the same period, and then throughout the 4th century BC. In both regions, the inlay technique was increasingly used and expanded into other materials: gold, silver, malachite, turquoise, jade or glass paste.

The smooth surface of this food-display vessel is inlaid with jumping wild animals pursued by hunters armed with bows and spears.

Some vessels, decorated with various ritual scenes divided into different registers, vividly evoke the life of the princes through archery (left, at the right-hand side, a wild goose hunt), dancing or music (left, at the left-hand side). It is also possible to see great drums and peals of stone gongs and bells without clappers, which were rung with a mallet. Other vessels display fantastic or masked creatures, half-human, half-animal (below).

The Chu tradition in the south

In 689 BC, the kingdom of Chu established its capital in the basin of the Blue River, near present-day Jiangling, in Hubei. After having conquered all neighbouring states, one after the other, it became the largest in all China, rivalling in splendour the princely courts of the valley of the Yellow River. The first archaeological discoveries occurred during the great works of modernization – in this case a railway line – that were carried out in the 1930s in the region of Changsha in Hunan. Since then, thousands of burials have been unearthed. However, it was the excavation of a tomb outside the actual domain of Chu that really revealed the different aspects of this original and profoundly Chinese culture.

The tomb of Marquis Yi of Zeng

The discovery of the tomb of Marquis Yi was made by
some soldiers who undertook the task of levelling the
summit of a small hill in Hubei in September 1977.
At a spot called Leigudun, they came across the top of
a pit that was 13 metres (42 feet) deep. Seven months
later, archaeologists unearthed the perfectly preserved
burial of a man aged forty-five, who died in 433 BC
and was carefully buried in a double coffin of lacquered
wood insulated from the walls of the pit by charcoal
and fine clay. It was the final resting place of the Marquis
Yi of Zeng, a mysterious little principality enclosed
within the heart of the kingdom of Chu, which would
have remained unknown, because there was no written

The peal of Marquis
Yi of Zeng (above)
comprised 65 bells
hanging on three levels.
Each of the bells bore
the name of its note,
and could produce two
sounds. The one in the
centre, almost a metre
high (over 3 feet) and
weighing more than 130
kilos (286 lbs) is one of
the largest ever found in
China.

evidence about it, had it not been for the inscriptions on the grave goods. This discovery revolutionized knowledge in fields as varied as funerary rites, weaponry, the history of music and metallurgical techniques.

'Where cultures meet'

In its structure as well as its grave goods, the tomb shows a unique combination of influences from China in the north and from Chu in the south. The care lavished on the insulation of the tomb reveals a new preoccupation with protecting the deceased; the halberdiers painted on the inner coffin are another manifestation of this concern. The very precise function allotted to each of its four chambers may also be regarded as foreshadowing tombs conceived as underground palaces. The central chamber is devoted to ritual – it is occupied by bronzes and the most extraordinary collection of musical instruments ever discovered in China: 124 instruments, bells, stone gongs, drums, lutes or zithers, mouth-organs or flutes, some of which were previously unknown. The marquis rests to the east, with his lacquered grave goods, while to the west there are the thirteen coffins of young sacrificed women and, to the north, a veritable

A tangle of creatures sprouts forth from the surface of the bronzes of Leigudun, giving them a baroque heaviness. The vessel above, cast with the usual technique of section-moulds, has decoration produced by the lost wax method.

The inner coffin of lacquered wood of Marquis Yi of Zeng is decorated with magical and religious motifs. On either side of a window, hybrid figures of horned bird-men and halberdier guards have a fantastic appearance that was probably intended to repel malevolent spirits. They must be seen as the coffin's protective divinities.

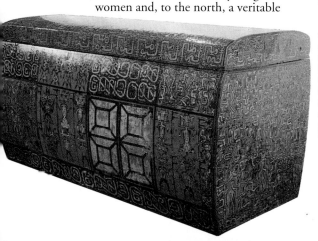

arsenal. Two hundred bamboo strips form an inventory of the presents offered to the deceased, and they record an impressive number of chariots, weapons and armour that were deployed at the funeral of the marquis. To judge by the magnificence of the 7000 objects deposited in his tomb (more than 10 tons of bronzes), he must have been both rich and powerful. These grave goods are representative of 5th-century BC production. The bronzes include some exceptional pieces. Some were produced using processes that were hitherto practically unknown in China, and which make possible some new effects of reticulated reliefs and sprouting interlace. These effects were obtained by soldering and by lost-wax casting, a process that consists of moulding clay around a wax model that melts when the metal is poured into the mould. This technique was invented in the Near East in the 4th millennium BC, and its use in China seems to date back to the 6th century BC, having probably been borrowed from the populations of the north.

Lacquer art, silk art, Chu art

The tomb of the marquis also contained more profane pieces. They are an indication of the profound changes that, at the end of the 5th and the beginning of the 4th century BC, brought about the decline of ritual bronzes.

Art on lacquer is particularly well represented here. The sign of a time when bronze was increasingly reserved for weapons, it was the great achievement of the kingdom of Chu. On the coffin, painted on a lacquer base, are the supernatural creatures of the inlaid bronzes of northern China,

The man riding a dragon (opposite) depicts the deceased in his ascension. It is a painting on silk from Changsha. The collar of the silk garment (centre) was found in a Chu tomb at Mashan (Hubei) that contained the body of a woman wrapped in thirteen layers of silk.

here probably linked to shamanism, which had a very strong hold in the south.

Chu is not only famous for its lacquerware, but also for its textiles – sumptuous silks, gauzes or embroideries. The two oldest known paintings on silk come from Chu; they were discovered in 1949 and 1973, and date back to the 4th–3rd century BC. They evoke the ascension of the deceased towards immortality, a new theme that was later developed in an important way by the Han.

Left: a map of the heavens painted on the lid of a clothes chest of lacquered wood. Framed by two fabulous animals, an inscription in small letters enumerates the 28 equatorial divisions (constellations), set out around a large central character that designates the Big Dipper. The *zhenmushou* in lacquered wood (left), a creature devouring a snake, is recognizable by its antler, its protruding eyes and its hanging tongue. This theme is linked to the protection of the dead, a preoccupation that continued to grow through the centuries.

4th–3rd century BC: on the way to a new world

In the north as in the south, the period of the 4th and 3rd centuries BC was devoted to the development of profane grave

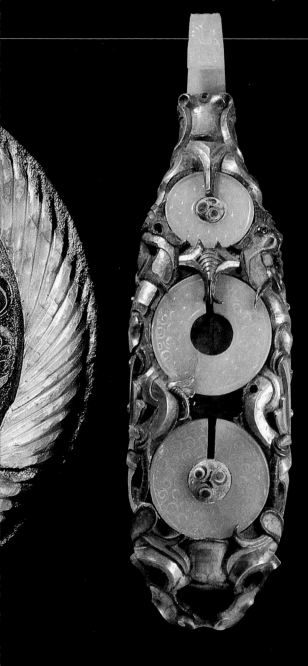

Eight tombs excavated at Jincun in Henan in 1928 are dated to the end of the Warring States (3rd century BC). They contained sophisticated grave goods that are difficult to classify from the present state of our knowledge. The exceptional quality of the objects, including the disk or mirror-back (far left), leads to the conclusion that they could have belonged to members of the royal family, and been made in a court workshop. Made of bronze, this work combines inlaid glass paste (including a bead in the centre) and pieces of jade, a quasi-constant reference to the past at the dawn of empire. The same idea is found in the belt buckle (left), which was unearthed in 1951 at Guweicun (Henan). The use of buckles, which was introduced in the north and north-west, spread through China in the period of the Eastern Zhou; it points to links with the nomadic world of Eurasia. At the same time, eye-shaped beads of glass paste appeared in the tombs, in imitation of Egyptian or Middle Eastern models.

goods. The tomb, symbol of a new elite, gradually became the manifestation of the deceased's personal accomplishments. The appearance of vast tree-covered tumuli above rich tombs, probably an idea borrowed from the world of the steppes, illustrates this evolution. It culminated, in the 3rd century BC, in the period of the first emperor.

In northern China, the tombs of Pingshan in Hebei are a good example. It was irrigation works that, in 1974, led archaeologists to the site, the last abode of

The motif of the winged feline (below, devouring a fawn) was borrowed from western Asia via the nomadic world.

the sovereigns of the kingdom of Zhongshan. Here they made the quite unprecedented discovery of a plaque of bronze, inlaid with gold and silver, which bore the plan of a funerary complex comprising five tombs and their temples. Two pits containing chariots and horses were found to the south. Another held boats.

Although it had been disturbed twice, the burial of King Cuo was filled with rich grave goods, including large tridents, probably insignia of power, and superb inlaid bronzes that contrasted with more austere pieces.

The lampbearer in court dress (opposite) is typical of the Warring States and the Han. Snakes make up the branches of the lamp, on which small monkeys are climbing.

These grave goods were representative of the new trends of the 4th century BC. During this period lamps and incense-burners were associated with wine vessels intended for banquets that no longer had any ceremonial aspect at all. Some of these lamps were made of terracotta and were not functional. They were *mingqi*, substitutes for purely funerary usage. Under the empire, they appeared frequently as evocations of the daily life of the deceased or, in more spectacular fashion, in the form of terracotta armies intended to protect him in the next world.

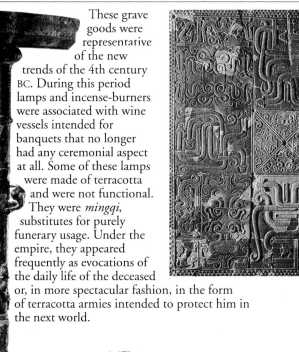

The *liubo* (above), a kind of back-gammon, was used with quoits and dice. It was a game of chance, sometimes used for divination. This specimen from Pingshan, made of stone and sumptuously decorated with intertwined snakes, is unique.

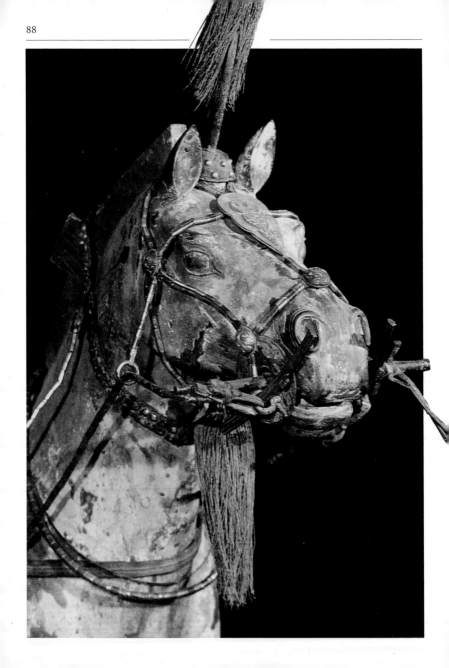

Qin, one of the mighty states fighting for supremacy, defeated its most powerful adversaries one after the other. In 221 BC King Zheng of Qin unified China and took the title of Qin Shi Huangdi, the 'first sovereign emperor'. The Chinese empire was born. It lasted until 1911.

CHAPTER 5

QIN OR THE FIRST EMPIRE

This little bronze tiger (right), a symbol of a country that was now under a single authority, was used by the emperor to control his army. The two halves were shared between the emperor and his generals. Imperial messages could only be guaranteed to be authentic if accompanied by the other half. Opposite: the head of a harnessed horse belonging to a bronze imperial quadriga.

These eave tiles (left), decorated with a toad and a deer, and the bronze beam-sockets (below) were discovered on a Qin palace site.

In the 8th century BC the first bronze coins, which replaced the traditional cowrie shells, were spade-shaped (opposite bottom). In the basin of the Yellow River, these spade coins remained the principal means of payment until the 3rd century BC. After the unification of China, *banliang* (round coins with a square hole), used in the kingdom of Qin, were imposed throughout the empire.

A new order after chaos

Before becoming an empire, Qin was a state in the west whose rise in power was probably due in large measure to its original and centralized administration that was set up in the 4th century BC by a movement of Legalist theoreticians. (Legalism held that people were naturally evil and needed to be controlled by fear.)

As soon as he took power, Qin Shi Huangdi began a series of radical reforms. A new administrative system was extended to the whole of the territory, which was divided into prefectures and districts run by civil servants who were paid by central government. Roads were built to facilitate the movement of troops. Laws were decreed. The different systems of writing were simplified, weights and measures standardized, opponents mercilessly eliminated. Thousands of men were deported and mobilized on gigantic works. It was at this time that the first sections of the Great Wall, simple fortifications of tamped earth, were built. It was a challenge to the 'barbarians' of the north and created a symbolic barrier between two worlds, the Chinese and the other. The first emperor, who wanted a sumptuous capital, settled at Xianyang, near present-day Xi'an, in Shaanxi.

According to Sima Qian, the famous Han historian, he built himself several residences there and magnificent palaces. Like his tomb, they were unfortunately ruined shortly after his death during the overthrow of his short-lived dynasty. In 1975

archaeologists only discovered the foundations of a vast brick edifice, which, for the first time in China, was built in several tiers. Of the palaces, only a few rooms remained, to which open galleries led, as well as tiles, small fragments of painted plaster, bricks and decorated floor tiles. However, the imperial funerary park had much more to offer.

Under the Qin, the western end of the Great Wall was in Inner Mongolia. Only a few sections from this period have been preserved, notably in the province of Ningxia (above).

The imperial mausoleum, centre of the world

Throughout his life, the emperor suffered from the fear of dying. On several occasions he sent messengers to the remote seas in search of islands, abodes of immortals who might possess an elixir of life. He died unexpectedly in 210 BC, only eleven years after he took power. More than 700,000 men, sentenced to hard labour, were used in the construction of his mausoleum, which had been begun at the start of his reign. Adopting the tradition of the ancient Qin, he chose to create a vast funerary park inside a double enclosure. The conception of the whole tomb reveals the megalomania of this man who wanted to initiate a new era. The enormous tumulus that rises above his tomb symbolized the centre of the world, personified by the emperor. Close by, Qin Shi Huangdi had a temple built, which he dedicated not to his ancestors but to himself. In this context, the interior of the burial vault could only be grandiose, and indeed it is, if the extraordinary account of Sima Qian is to be believed. The emperor's final abode, a gigantic underground palace, was also meant to be a representation of the universe: 'Mercury was used to make the hundred rivers and the vast sea.... High up were all the constellations of the heavens; below, the whole geographical layout of the earth.' Today it still retains an air of mystery. Out of fear, perhaps, of only finding ruins, the mausoleum – which was

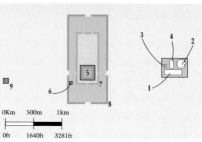

The tumulus (5) that covers the imperial mausoleum stands near Lintong, in Shaanxi, 35 kilometres (21 miles) east of Xi'an. It is surrounded by two rectangular enclosures (7, 8). The workers' tombs (9) have been found to the west, as well as two bronze quadrigas (6). The four pits containing the terracotta army are located on the eastern side (1, 2, 3, 4), about 1 kilometre (over half a mile) outside the enclosure. The discovery of these pits gave rise to restoration work that was unprecedented in China (opposite).

declared a historical monument in 1961 – has not yet been excavated. Only the surrounding area has been explored by archaeologists.

An unprecedented discovery

In accordance with the emperor's wishes, the tumulus resembles a mountain, larger than the biggest Egyptian pyramid. In the surrounding area, a few modest discoveries were made at first, though it was not until March 1974 that a truly remarkable find, one of the greatest archaeological discoveries in China, was unearthed by chance. At a distance of 1200 metres (nearly 4000 feet) to the east of the outer enclosure of the tumulus, peasants digging a well hit the top of an underground construction strewn with debris of terracotta. A team of archaeologists was immediately sent to the spot. Thousands of terracotta warriors soon sprang out of the burnt debris of a timber structure, aligned in eleven rows more than 200 metres (650 feet) long.

The squadron of armoured infantrymen (left) is preceded by two charioteers with outstretched arms. The height, uniform and hairstyle of the warriors vary according to their rank. They are equipped with a breastplate worn on a leather or felt coat that protects the lower part of their body, a tunic, breeches and leggings. Their feet rest on pedestals. Their hair is pulled back, plaited and raised on top of the skull in a wide variety of ways. The officers wear a headband (below) or a headdress.

Two quadrigas (half life-size) in polychrome bronze (left) were discovered in 1980, to the west of the tumulus, and with them one of the oldest complete harnesses ever found in China — one with leather straps of a kind that only appeared ten centuries later in the West. These quadrigas have been admirably restored (below). The first is a closed ceremonial chariot with doors and windows. The bodywork of bamboo, wood and leather is covered in metal and decorated with gold and silver. The driver, sitting on his heels, holds the reins. The second is an open type of chariot. An oval canopy with an umbrella-like structure protects the driver.

A gigantic project of excavation, analysis and restoration began, which still continues today to the fascination of the public. The place has become a museum, and each year attracts millions of visitors from all over the world, who find here an echo of the fantastic evocations of the texts. This highly symbolic excavation site has become China's cultural showcase.

An army for eternity

In 1976 the discovery of three new pits revealed the headquarters of this army of the shadows, with detachments of chariots and cavalry. More than 6000 warriors in battle formation have been unearthed, depicting the famous army, which, as an instrument of his supremacy, was intended to protect the emperor in the afterlife. Like the straw or wooden mannequins placed in the tombs of the Eastern Zhou from the 6th century BC onwards, these clay statues replaced the sacrificial victims of the Shang and Zhou. Such *mingqi,* figurines specially manufactured for funerary use, were later widely adopted, though never on such a monumental scale as the Qin soldiers who, according to their rank, measure between 175 cm (68⅞") and 196 cm (77⅛"). Although the infantry comprise a large part of the army, some pits also contained generals and senior officers, cavalry standing next to their mounts, charioteers and chariots and crouching archers. Even though they are represented in a slightly wooden way,

R eal bronze weapons were found with the emperor's clay soldiers: spears, pikes, long swords or axe-daggers (left, crossbow bolts).

Colours were applied to the statues after firing. This treatment made it possible to identify the various units of this army (through their yellow, green, red, black, white or purple uniform). Traces of pigments found on some statues have helped in experiments to restore their original appearance (opposite, an archer). Left: the head of a warrior being excavated. Below: a detail of a hand.

these sculptures reveal a totally new means of artistic expression. Originally they were painted and had real bronze weapons, notably crossbows, which were invented later in the West, but which date back in China to the beginning of the Warring States. Despite their individualized appearance, these statues, which were made from several moulds, testify to a process of mass-production that required the existence of workshops organized on a quasi-industrial scale. Other remains have been discovered, close to the imperial tumulus, but the site has certainly not yet revealed all of its secrets.

In 210 BC the death of the first emperor brought about the fall of the Qin. The troubles that followed did not die down until 206 BC, when a rebel peasant, Liu Bang, founded the Han dynasty and restored the feudal system.

The Han reigned for four hundred years, an eventful period that had a profound effect on the history of China. It was characterized not only by expeditions to Central Asia, merchants on the Silk Road, zealous civil servants, erudite emperors, but also by social unrest and rebellions. Far from the Roman empire, which was blossoming to the West, the Chinese empire expanded to the East.

CHAPTER 6
THE SPREAD OF THE HAN EMPIRE

From the idealized classicism inherited from the Qin (opposite, funerary figurine from the mausoleum of the emperor Jingdi in Shaanxi) to the liveliness of the end of the dynasty (right, exorcist statuette discovered in Sichuan), the Han mode of depiction is an expressive art.

An archaeology of tombs

Without a doubt the Han period was one of the most dazzling eras in Chinese history, a fact reflected in its archaeological remains. However, owing to the scarcity of discoveries and the lack of interest in habitation sites on the part of Chinese researchers, the archaeology of this period is primarily an archaeology of tombs. The change of dynasty does not mark a break; at the end of the 3rd century BC, and until the reign of Wudi (140 BC), China inherited traditions that had been developed under the Warring States.

The north preserved the Qin custom of digging around the tumulus pits that were filled with a guard for the afterlife. In one example, at Yangjiawan in Shaanxi, the figurines do not exceed 60 cm (23⅝") in height. In contrast, the south remained strongly influenced by the traditions of the ancient kingdom of Chu. The tomb of the Marquise of Dai, found in 1971 at Mawangdui, close to Changsha in Hunan, is the most representative of this period.

The voyage of the soul

Constructed at the bottom of a pit that was almost 20 metres (65 feet) long and partitioned, the burial was

Left: lacquerware toilet box from Mawangdui.

accessible down a sloping ramp. Its central plan and the concern for protecting the tomb and its occupant are characteristic features of the early Han. This preoccupation was based on new beliefs: people are endowed with two souls, *po* and *hun*, which separate at the moment of death. The *po* soul, which animates the body, wanders the underground world, while the *hun*, the spiritual soul, flies off to attain immortality. This perilous ascension is evoked by a painted silk banner placed on the coffin. These banners or 'clothes for taking flight' were used for the rite of recalling the soul before they were buried during the funeral. The deceased's environment also had to contribute to this transition which, if successful, would make him or her a benevolent ancestor.

Protecting the body of the deceased

Particular care was devoted to the construction, to making it watertight, and to the interior layout of the pit. The central compartment contained four nested coffins of lacquered wood decorated with mythological figures, birds, animals and beings of good omen, which were thought to create a protective environment of symbols and divinities around the deceased so that she could enter into communication with the next world. Her body was embalmed. Wrapped in twenty layers of clothing, it was found intact, soaked in a bactericidal liquid.

The tomb's grave goods show the same concern for ensuring the well-being of the deceased, who was buried with reserves of food and clothes. An inventory was drawn up and listed on bamboo slips. Among the most precious objects were pieces of lacquerware, more valuable than the bronzes, and some superb silks.

The three stages of the world are depicted on the Mawangdui banner (opposite), one of the rare paintings preserved from the period:

the underground world (the 'yellow springs'), the world of humans and the celestial world, the end of the journey on which she was accompanied by her attendants, figurines of painted wood (above).

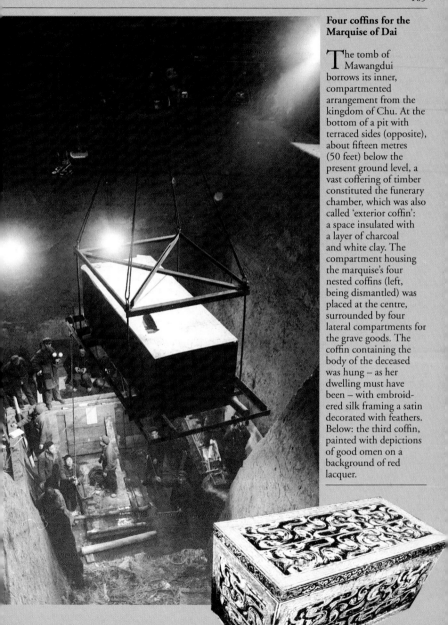

Four coffins for the Marquise of Dai

The tomb of Mawangdui borrows its inner, compartmented arrangement from the kingdom of Chu. At the bottom of a pit with terraced sides (opposite), about fifteen metres (50 feet) below the present ground level, a vast coffering of timber constituted the funerary chamber, which was also called 'exterior coffin': a space insulated with a layer of charcoal and white clay. The compartment housing the marquise's four nested coffins (left, being dismantled) was placed at the centre, surrounded by four lateral compartments for the grave goods. The coffin containing the body of the deceased was hung – as her dwelling must have been – with embroidered silk framing a satin decorated with feathers. Below: the third coffin, painted with depictions of good omen on a background of red lacquer.

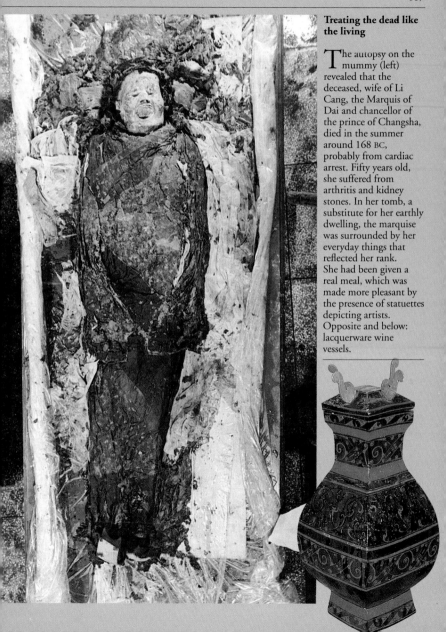

Treating the dead like the living

The autopsy on the mummy (left) revealed that the deceased, wife of Li Cang, the Marquis of Dai and chancellor of the prince of Changsha, died in the summer around 168 BC, probably from cardiac arrest. Fifty years old, she suffered from arthritis and kidney stones. In her tomb, a substitute for her earthly dwelling, the marquise was surrounded by her everyday things that reflected her rank. She had been given a real meal, which was made more pleasant by the presence of statuettes depicting artists. Opposite and below: lacquerware wine vessels.

An underground house

In northern China, the evolution in tombs begun in the 4th century BC continued. The funerary chamber, first constructed simply at the bottom of the pit, was later moved to one of its sides. Its walls were soon fitted out with large hollow bricks, a formula already adopted by the first emperor for the decoration of his palaces. In this way it was possible to overcome the lack of timber caused by extensive deforestation. From the 2nd century BC onwards, this small chamber, at first cubic with a flat roof, became a real house with a door, a gabled roof and pediments. An annexe-chamber was sometimes built at one side. Others were later added as it became customary under the emperor Wudi (140–87 BC) to bury couples in the same tomb.

These tombs were constructed of large hollow bricks, which were decorated, and small solid bricks, which were less heavy, making more flexible constructions possible. Stamped or painted, they depict both secular themes – carts or hunts – and themes of religious

Throughout China tombs gradually began to be constructed on an axial plan, typically used for the tombs of the middle classes of low-ranking officials, landowners and rich peasants (left, tomb no. 61 at Luoyang in Henan). The pediment is decorated using the theme of the exorcist, a sort of monster surmounted by a large bird (above centre). On the sides, immortals and auspicious animals (deer, dragon, tiger and phoenix) ensure the tomb's protection. The painting of the lintel, which illustrates an edifying story, reflects the development, in the first century AD, of the Confucian philosophy, which laid emphasis on filial piety and social conformity.

inspiration linked to the reception and protection of the deceased, or to his ascension towards immortality: exorcists, guardians or auspicious animals. From the 1st century BC onwards, scenes of festivities, a projection of the life desired for the deceased, also appeared, together with portraits and historical evocations of didactic or moral value.

The first stone sculptures date to the same period, but most of those that have been found are more recent. The oldest to survive, the horse crushing a 'barbarian' discovered by Segalen near Xi'an in Shaanxi, is dated to 117 BC.

The palatial sculpture of the Han has not survived. Only a few stone sculptures remain, marking the 'spirit

roads' in funerary parks: an avenue bordered with statues, stelae and pillars leading to the offerings chamber built in front of the tumulus.

Those pictured above and left, albeit still very crude, are among the oldest known. They were associated with the tomb of General Huo Qubing (140–117 BC).

The reign of Wudi or the Han empire at its height

In the 2nd century BC the empire entered a phase of technical progress and of great expansion. The emperor sent emissaries to Central Asia, followed by costly military expeditions to bring back to China the famous stallions of Ferghana, with which he hoped to equip his cavalry. He successfully overcame the Xiongnu nomads and expanded the empire's territory in all directions, from Central Asia to Korea and Vietnam. Research carried out by Chinese archaeologists following the work of Sven Hedin or Aurel Stein at Xinjiang and Gansu led to the discovery of the ancient lines of defence and the military establishments set up to protect and organize these frontier regions. The expansion westwards encouraged trade all along the Silk Road and indirectly established the first contacts between Rome and Chang'an, the Chinese capital.

Chang'an, the lost capital

This expansion helped to develop an urban civilization which gave court life tremendous prominence. However, today only a few ruins remain to mark the former splendour of Chang'an, the prestigious capital built in the

The dynasty's two main preoccupations were maintaining contact with Central Asia, a crucial region for the development of trade on the Silk Road, and containing the nomads of the empire's northern confines, as the above watchtower shows. Yet the animal art of the steppes (left) influenced Han artistic expression. The figurines of the imperial mausoleum of Jingdi (far left and opposite page above and below) retain the rigidity of the Qin soldiers. Their arms, made of wood, could not be moved.

3rd century BC near Xi'an. The archaeological study of the site began in 1956, when part of its tamped-earth enclosure was found. Since then, its streets and its palaces have been excavated, and an armoury and two ceremonial sites have been located. However, the sumptuous decoration that adorned the palaces has not survived. Little more is known of the eleven imperial mausoleums grouped to the north of the Wei River – none of them has yet been opened.

The tumuli, whose beneficial location had been carefully determined by geomancers, stand on a tree-covered terrace. Each of them had its own funerary park, with an entrance flanked by two towers bearing the name of the deceased, which today are known to us only from depictions on stamped bricks. In the surrounding area real towns grew up, inhabited by rich families entrusted with the upkeep of the park.

Mancheng, the pomp of the princes

Fortunately, several tombs that belonged to princes or members of the imperial family have been excavated. They provide valuable information about the sumptuous art of the court. The tombs of Liu Sheng – ninth son of the emperor Jingdi, who died in 113 BC, and of his wife Dou Wan, who died in 104 BC – were discovered during the summer of 1968 at Mancheng in Hebei, about 150 kilometres (90 miles) from Beijing. They are among the rare sites that were dug during the Cultural Revolution.

The tomb at Mancheng (above) contained a 'reception room' with chariots and horses to the side and, at the back, the burial chamber, the prince's 'private apartment'.

These twin tombs, which had not been disturbed, were dug into a rocky cliff. Conceived on an axial plan, they reveal the Han concern for arranging their tombs like real buildings. This vast palace reproduced a structure of wood and tiles. It was approached by an avenue.

The deceased rested in lacquered and inlaid coffins, dressed in a jade 'shroud', a kind of sarcophagus comprising more than 2000 jade wafers sewn together with golden thread, intended to protect the body from decay and to enable it to reach the paradise of the immortals. It provides the first archaeological evidence of a phenomenon mentioned by the texts that reflects the first emperor's quest for immortality with the help of drugs sought 'beyond the seas' among the immortals. The appearance in the tombs of incense-burners in the form of mountains evokes the abode of those mythical creatures, who also began to be depicted. Other shrouds have subsequently been discovered. In more modest tombs, it sufficed to seal the orifices of the dead with small jade amulets.

Precious collections

The grave goods in the two tombs, comprising 2800 objects, are particularly impressive. The bronzes are of exceptional quality, in accordance with the rank of the deceased. Alongside undecorated pieces, which became typical from the 2nd century BC onwards, some vessels were inlaid with gold and silver thread. These pieces from the collection provide information on the movement of objects, gifts received from other courts, ancient pieces passed down as legacies, or exotic objects brought back from abroad. The tomb of the second king of Nanyue, a small kingdom in the Canton region, also includes pieces from the steppes, at the other end of China, and even from Iran or Hellenistic Central Asia.

The quality of the jade, associated with the princely tombs, from the tomb of the second king of Nanyue makes this disk (below) one of the most outstanding pieces discovered so far. Bottom: the jade shroud of Liu Sheng and his headrest.

Above left: an amulet in the form of a cicada.

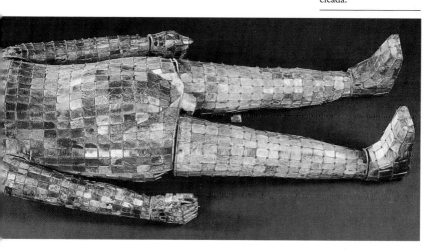

The Eastern Han: new values, a humanized art

The end of the 1st century BC was marked by tensions, not only at court but also in the countryside. The peasants were suppressed by the great landowners, while the upper classes indulged in a wide variety of entertainments. The period from 50 BC to AD 50 constitutes a decisive turning point for this society that was in the process of change.

In the year AD 9, Wang Meng, a member of an illustrious family, took advantage of the political troubles to usurp the throne. However, in AD 25, the Han, who had left Chang'an in Shaanxi, succeeded in

The most widespread tomb type in the first century is a kind of hypogeum with a high vaulted ceiling (below) comprising several chambers of small, solid bricks – a material that made it possible to extend spatially and produce more flexible and complex structures than the large hollow bricks used during the Western Han.

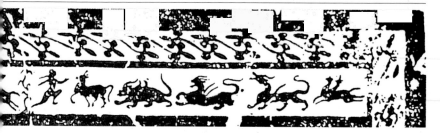

regaining control of the situation. Guang Wudi, who established the capital further east at Luoyang in Henan, became the first of the Eastern Han emperors. From this point on there were two Han dynasties: Western Han and Eastern Han, which ended in AD 220. Once again, funerary architecture reflects these changes.

Towards the mid-1st century AD, the ancestral cult for each emperor was transferred to the temple inside the mausoleum. At the same time, for the rich, the tomb became an open place where nearest and dearest could gather. For the living, it became not only a means of displaying their virtue and their filial piety, but also a way of showing off their wealth, for which they incurred enormous expenses. The 2nd century was a golden age for funerary art. After this period, the decorative tradition found at the beginning of Han period was replaced by a figurative art. There was a move away from the fantastic towards the representation of a real, humanized world. It was no longer the voyage of the soul that was of interest, but life *post mortem*, transposition of the world of the living.

The exemplary life of a high-ranking official

In Inner Mongolia, near Helinger, the tomb of a high-ranking official – who died around 170, but whose name remains unknown despite numerous inscriptions – is an outstanding illustration of this change.

Inside the tombs, the decoration of the lintels varies from region to region. The most common themes are hunting scenes (above, tomb 4 of Mizhi in Shaanxi).

With its curly hair and its non-Chinese face, the lampbearer below could depict a foreigner from Southeast Asia.

From the private apartments to the outhouses for the carriages, the wealth of the domain of Helinger in Inner Mongolia is depicted very vividly in its owner's tomb. Each painting evokes the different aspects of life in the country, from cooking or banquets to work in the fields, from the gathering of mulberry leaves to the threshing of grain, not forgetting the cowshed or the stable, the pigsty and the sheepfold, the wells, the furnaces or the meat reserves. Horses (left) played an important role in this world. Looked after carefully, broken in and trained, they were regularly inspected by civil servants. Since the time of Wudi, who had introduced the big stallions from the West in order to reinforce his army and fight the nomads by beating them at their own game, governmental pastures had been created on the confines of the empire, in the frontier regions of the north and west.

At Helinger some scenes evoke the public life of civil servants, recognizable by the circular canopy above their chariots (left). Since the time of Wudi, their importance had continually grown, as the emperor had built for himself a new administration intended to neutralize the influence of a troublesome nobility. For this purpose, he created schools for producing the future Confucian scholars.

The decoration, which is entirely painted and annotated, retraces the main events of his career, from his first nomination to his last title of 'colonel-protector of the Wuhuan'. Each image depicts his official dwellings, with vehicles, horses and all the honours that it was hoped the deceased would find in the next world. The civil servant's retreat in the hills and pastures of his domain is also evoked by a series of tableaux illustrating the deceased's worldly wealth. This theme was very much in fashion during this period, when cities were beginning to lose their importance as immense self-sufficient domains developed and landownership increased.

Funerary art, popular art

Life on the estates is also evoked by the *mingqi,* figurines that were specially manufactured for funerary use. They illustrate the development of a completely new popular art, a specifically funerary art that, for the first time, concentrated on daily life. The tombs contain not only servants, dancers or musicians but also horses, domestic animals, models of granaries, furnaces or pigsties, farms or elegant pavilions that evoke country life.

Like the paintings of Helinger, the terracotta models of watchtowers (left), in vogue at the end of Han, are evidence for the increase in the number of fiefs, faced with a central power in crisis. They illustrate the development of great domains, guarded by armed militias. These miniature constructions also reveal the period's architecture of wood and cob – today only tiles and eaves survive.

The number and quality of the *mingqi*, which were mass-produced, varied in accordance with the status of the deceased. Some, like the bronze 'flying horse' found in the tomb of a general buried at Leitai in Gansu (centre), are real masterpieces. With one hoof poised on a flying bird, it evokes 'the celestial horses with blood for sweat', those proud steeds from the West which, three centuries earlier, the emperor Wudi had brought back from Ferghana.

The meaning of the concrete

The stamped decoration in light relief gives the funerary bricks of Sichuan a particular style. Mass-produced, they illustrate scenes of daily life – harvesting, hunting wild geese, salt extraction, rice planting, or distillation and transportation of alcohol (left). By contrast, the erotic scene (overleaf) is very rare. The four people (three men with erections and a woman) seem to have hung their clothes on the branch of a tree in which small monkeys are climbing. The naturalistic treatment of the landscape is an innovation of this period. Below: a man made out of bronze working a grinder.

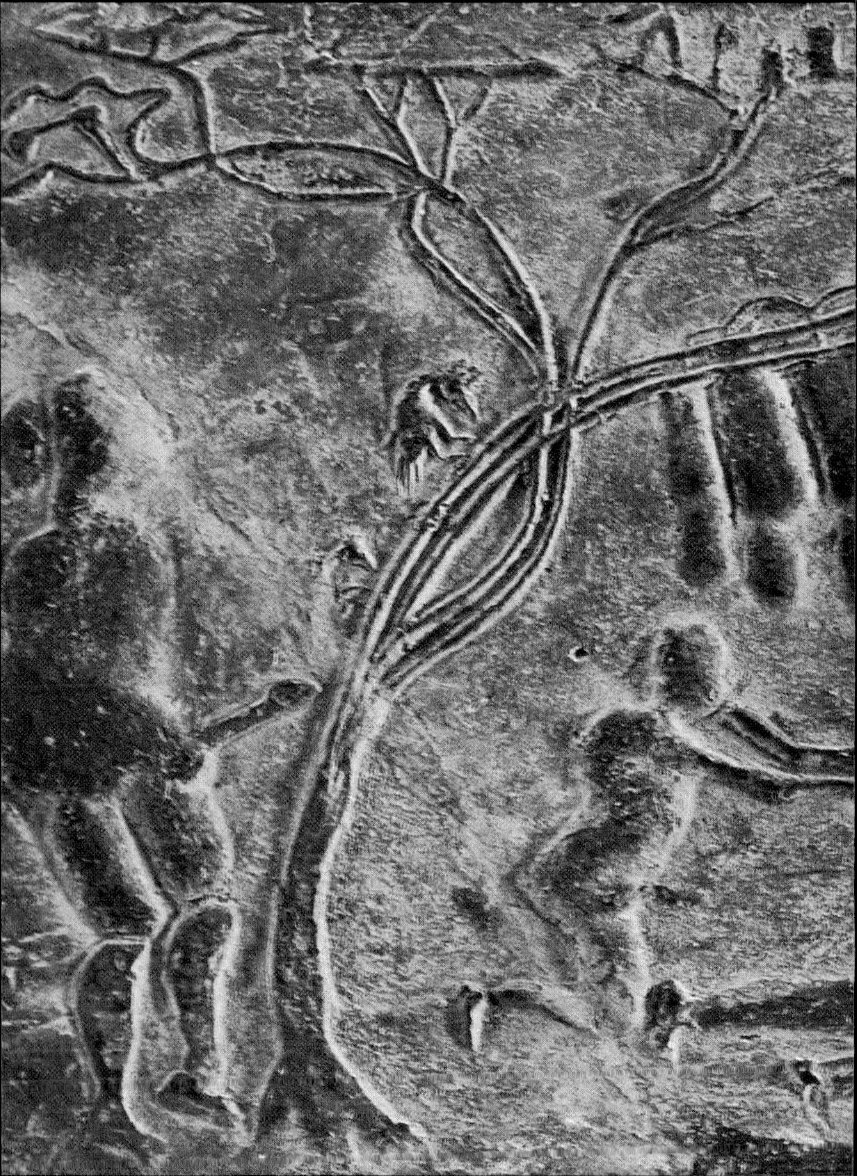

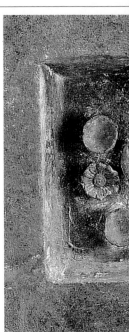

This development of the *mingqi* has to be linked with the search for cheap substitutes for rare or expensive products that were reserved for the elite: ceramics covered in a green glaze or stoneware with a brown covering imitate bronze; glass imitates jade, while painted pots also try to equal a declining lacquerware art.

Regional craftwork

The weakening of central power encouraged the expansion of the great domains, though it also caused the regions to turn in on themselves, resulting in the development of regional craftwork. In northern China, solid bricks were sometimes associated with stone slabs with chiselled decoration, and the ceiling of tombs was decorated with stone beams held up by columns covered with complex corbels, faithful copies of wooden frameworks. However, it was often around the really heavy doors, which had piers and were surmounted by a lintel, that the use of stone was concentrated. Stone carving blossomed because of the progress in iron and steel technology.

In Henan, Shandong, Sichuan and Shaanxi, stone was also widely used outside tombs. Two towers inscribed with the deceased's name and titles marked the

Life in the country is widely represented in tombs by many figurines and small models that evoke a carefree existence. Above: a terracotta model of a rectangular reservoir, with a boat, ducks, fish and aquatic plants. Left: latrines, reached by a staircase, are located upstairs, above the pigsty.

This painted terracotta tambourine player (below) is part of a series of figurines of comic actors and storytellers from tombs in the Chengdu region of Sichuan (2nd century). Their features – displaying a mastery of space, expression, vigour, a sense of movement and humour – are characteristic of this region's workshops at the end of Han. Like the acrobats (opposite), he evokes the pleasures of entertainment so much appreciated at this time.

entrance of the funerary park. Winged felines were generally placed in front of them. Since the great palatial sculpture of the Han – whose existence is known from texts – has disappeared, these funerary sculptures are the only surviving evidence of Han statuary. In front of the tumulus there was a pavilion built of stone slabs. It had an open facade and served as an offerings chamber.

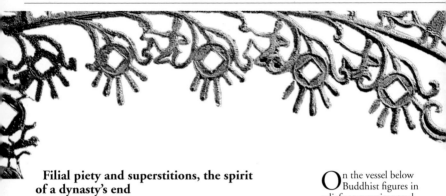

Filial piety and superstitions, the spirit of a dynasty's end

Archaeolgoical excavations have helped to build a much clearer picture of Han architecture and iconography and of the evolution of Han society.

The most famous architectural ensemble, and the only one to have survived intact, remains the Wu family mausoleum in Shandong. Dating to 150, it was discovered in the 11th century. The decoration has been worn away by numerous rubbings and so is less legible today than before. Nevertheless, the bas-reliefs that adorned the offerings chamber constructed by Wu Liang Ci, a retired scholar, still provide important evidence, as they represent in codified form the new cult of filial piety and shed light on a society that was highly structured, with a strong sense of universal order and people's place in it. This philosophy was particularly evident in that region of Shandong where the ancient kingdom of Lu was located, as it was the birthplace of Confucius.

Each part of the edifice corresponded to a different theme. The walls of the small room are an

On the vessel below Buddhist figures in relief are superimposed on the painted depictions of immortals. The new religion, at first considered an exotic variation on Chinese cults, was introduced in the 1st century in the Han empire via foreign merchants. It only really began to flourish as an independent church in the 4th century AD.

evocation of the earthly world. The ceiling, which conventionally symbolizes the heavens, is decorated with auspicious signs. These fashionable marks of approval sent by the heavens to the sovereign played a large role in Han thought. Signs of good omen, they enabled people to cling to the idea of a happy life in an attempt to avert the crisis that was gnawing away at Han society.

The money trees (detail, left) are typical objects of south-west China. Symbols of eternal health, they owe their name to the round coins that were hung in their branches.

A society in crisis

These efforts to ward off the uncertainties of the time did not prevent the collapse of the dynasty. From the 2nd century onwards, the authority of the imperial institution was damaged by the conflicts of interest between eunuchs, aristocratic families and scholars, while the rural world suffered from destitution.

Peasant revolts, uprisings and the growing power of the generals gradually degenerated into civil war.

In 220 one of these generals seized power and founded a short-lived dynasty in the north of the country. The fall of the Han resulted in the disintegration of the empire. China now entered a period of profoundly troubled times, lasting more than three centuries, sometimes called the Chinese Middle Ages: it was an era marked by instability and invasions by nomadic populations, during which six dynasties and three kingdoms followed one another. Eventually the country emerged totally transformed.

Above: a section of the stone relief from the Wu Liang Ci shrine showing edifying scenes taken from history.

Overleaf: the Great Wall of China.

DOCUMENTS

The time of the collectors

In the 19th century a huge antiquities market developed. There were numerous collectors both in China and abroad. Traders and art lovers displayed their collections, and soon scholars also ventured into this territory. Museums themselves sent emissaries, bought objects and financed expeditions. Andersson bought ceramics, then gave up the practice when he noticed that this trade was encouraging the looting of tombs by workers organized into rival gangs. From 1906 onwards, it became illegal to export important objects.

Théodore Duret and Henri Cernuschi search for bronzes

Having made a collection of Japanese bronzes in Japan, we immediately set about collecting Chinese bronzes on arriving in China....

Trade in curiosities, bronzes, porcelains, jades, cloisonnés is carried out in China by people who know the exact age, style and value of the objects they possess. When a rare piece appears at a trader's, all the enthusiasts are immediately aware of it. Although we are not talking about an auction house, the traders are extremely good at making the enthusiasts compete with one another. The Chinese enthusiasts and the staff of the European legations who, in their boredom, spend their time collecting, are thus very often rivals....

In Peking [Beijing] we cannot operate as we did in Yedo [Tokyo], where we bought bronzes outright by the hundreds. Most of the time we have to buy the pieces one by one, after long bargaining, and in the end there is always a high price to pay for them....

Collecting in Peking [Beijing] demands a certain amount of relevant knowledge. The objects are classified according to their marks and their inscriptions, by dynasties and by the emperors' reigns.... In order to collect bronzes in particular, it is necessary to obtain certain books that deal with the subject. These books are in the hands of the principal dealers, who use them as a vade mecum. They are: the *Pou-Kou-Tou (Bogotulu), Figures of a Great Number of Antiquities*, published for the first time in the Soung [Song] dynasty, around AD 1200, and reprinted several times since; the *Si-Tching-Kou-Kieng, Memoir on the Antiquities of Western Purity*, which is the descriptive catalogue of the collection of ancient bronzes assembled by Emperor Kieng-Long [Qianlong]; finally the *Tsi-Kou-Tchaï*, a more recent work by a viceroy of Canton [Guangzhou]....

Chinese bronzes date back to the remotest antiquity...they bear inscriptions in almost hieroglyphic characters that ceased to be used a long time ago, but books give their transcription in modern characters. The vessels of the Chang [Shang] dynasty, being the oldest, are the most valued by connoisseurs.

Théodore Duret
Voyage en Asie, 1874

Letter by Victor Segalen after the discovery of the tomb of Huo Qubing

From a distance one can see that this mound is topped not only by 'standing stones' but also by a temple, whose buildings rise in tiers on its north side. I have never encountered a tumulus like it. At some distance I saw the robust shape of a stone horse, and I rushed towards it. There was no doubt, its lines were far more archaic and more massive than those of Tang horses, and in a different style; it forms a block, and is not hollowed out under the belly. Above all, it is not just a horse that is sculpted here, but, against all expectations, a remarkably successful group: a horse, naked, trampling a man – his enormous, hairy head is visible between its front legs; his knees are bent beneath the beast's belly, and his toes are clutching both sides of the tail. His left hand still grasps the bow, which has the well-known double-curved shape – the Mongolian bow – while his right hand holds a short pike that is stuck into the beast's belly.

I admit that at first I associated these poses, this combat, and this subject with

Tomb of Huo Qubing.

the numerous episodes of struggle and ferocity that can be found in Chaldeo-Assyrian, Persian and Sassanid statuary. However, the history of the dead person enclosed beneath this tomb suffices, I think, to warrant this choice of subject: there can be no better celebration of a brilliant and ferocious cavalry general, always victorious, and doubtless killed in battle, than this heavy, powerful horse crushing a Hiong-nou [Xiongnu] barbarian.... Because the man displays all the features that Chinese artists attributed to the Huns: large head, prominent moustache, stocky body.... Finally, western influence, if there had been any, would no doubt have been shown above all in the face, the characteristic stylization of the beard.... But not a bit of it. The enormous mask seen upside down between the front hooves does not bring to mind any such thing. The beard stretches out in a new, very powerful, very decorative way against the horse's breast. I therefore conclude that the choice of subject is free of any influence from Asia Minor. Close examination of the statue shows that it has suffered a little: its contours are worn, eroded, and it is covered by a yellowish-white lichen. The south side (right) appears intact; the north side is much more affected. I do not know if it stood on a base, because the hooves and the base of the sculpted block are level with the ground.

This statue is in no way gigantic; from the ground to the ears it is only 1 m 40 [55"]. However, it has a powerful effect. For a start, the sculptor seems to have avoided any idea of copying or clichés. He did not try either to save himself trouble or to push his work too far. The horse, carved fully in the round, certainly crushes its human base, yet this flattened figure remains vigorous. The toes clutching the flat part of the tail form a posterior pillar, which, like the large upside-down head at the front, produces an effect without comparison in other statues.

This statue can be dated exactly to the death of Ho K'iu-ping [Huo Qubing], that is 117 BC. Its authenticity, it seems to me, can be established as follows....

The texts and the find are in perfect agreement. To the south of the tumulus a fine Kien long [Qianlong] stela, photographed at the same time as the horse, bears this inscription: (*Han hiao-k'i tsiang-kiun ta-sseu-ma Kouan-kiun heou Ho kong K'iu-ping mou*). Moreover, this tomb is part of the immense 'cemetery' of the Western Han. Finally, the very style of the statue makes it impossible to attach it to anything later than the Christian era. Besides, the complete study of the mound and the stone blocks on its summit and flanks confirms the preceding data. This tumulus, unlike the hundreds we have recorded, recognized and studied between Lin-t'ong [Lintong] and Hing-ping [Xingping], is the only one that is

topped by a stone construction that must have been colossal: rounded granite blocks, the smallest of which measures 2.5 to 3 m [8 to over 9 feet], are strewn over its sides and seem to have collapsed from the highest point....

In short, the tumulus of Ho K'iu-ping [Huo Qubing] appears to me to have been the location and the subject of some formidable architectural and sculptural work that I still cannot explain (why this ox halfway up the slope, these semi-flattened blocks?), but I intend to investigate this more thoroughly. I am making these projects the subject of a report to the French minister at Peking [Beijing].

It seems to me at present that the Chinese government would not have any objection to excavations that would be certain to produce evidence for a past that it does not renounce, because, despite the Revolution, Confucianism is regaining favour everywhere. Above all I feel that this statue of a 'naked horse trampling a Hiong-nou [Xiongnu] barbarian' would in no way be a disgrace to the Louvre's Chinese collections, where it could justifiably be placed on the grounds of its original and powerful style and its date....

Yours sincerely, my dear master,

Victor Segalen
to Edouard Chavannes
6 March 1914

P. S. In the monthly article that I write for *Le Temps*, I have been careful not to mention the exact location or even the name of the tumulus. The European dealers, not to mention the Japanese, are a cause of alarm. I therefore request that you maintain the same discretion in relation to the public. Moreover, the place is far less important here than the date.

Archaeologists and antiquarians

Every day there came to my house three or four different groups [of merchants] selling urns, and there was endless bargaining, whilst frequently in a single day thirty-odd urns or more would pass through my hands. I soon understood, however, that the various sellers had formed a syndicate, the members of which had undertaken not to accept any reduction in prices. I felt as if I stood before an insurmountable wall, and my money melted away with alarming rapidity.... My house was positively besieged by groups of men wanting to sell me urns....

Owing to the demand which we had created for these prehistoric relics, the Mohammedans had collected them in their hundreds in the old cemeteries. They had dug planlessly right and left, and when different parties came into conflict they had fought regular battles, in which one day a man with a spade had struck off the hand of his opponent. The consequence had been that the official in charge of the district in question had sent soldiers to see that no further excavations were made.

I now clearly understood that as a result of our purchases a most deplorable spoliation of graves in these prehistoric cemeteries had taken place, and in order to do what I could to prevent further violation I visited the governor and suggested that he should instruct the local authorities to see that the local population should not commit further outrages against these precious scientific monuments of ancient civilizations....

It soon became clear to me how many hundreds of graves containing burial ware of unique size and beauty had been looted by a desecration which had for all time rendered impossible a scientific investigation of the connection between the various objects in the graves....

For a long time we sought for graves which had escaped the ravages of the villagers. For several days it looked as if the whole district had been completely plundered, but finally Chuang made a magnificent discovery at Pien Chia Kou.

J. G. Andersson,
'Prehistory of the Chinese' in
*Bulletin of the Museum of Far Eastern
Antiquities*, XV, 1943

J ohan Gunnar Andersson in Stockholm.

The first emperor

The historian Sima Qian paints an unflattering portrait of Qin Shi Huangdi in terms of both his physique and his morals. He painstakingly describes the sovereign's grandiose mausoleum, but does not say a word about the emperor's clay warriors. The tombs of the workers who were sacrificed have been discovered. Archaeologists have recently found mercury close to the unexcavated tumulus. There is still an air of mystery surrounding this emperor, whose reign was extremely brief. It is thought that his capital and tomb were sacked shortly after his death...

Wei Liao, one of Qin Shi Huangdi's advisers, described him thus: 'He has the proboscis of a hornet and large all-seeing eyes. His chest is like that of a bird of prey and his voice like that of a jackal. He is merciless, with the heart of a tiger or a wolf.'

The mausoleum of the first emperor, a vast production

More than seven hundred thousand men who had undergone the punishment of castration were then sent, some to construct the Ngo-pang [Oubang] palace, others to construct (the tomb of) Mount Li. From the northern mountains a stone sarcophagus was taken; then timbers for construction from the lands of Chou [Chu] and King [Jing] were transported by floating, and all (these timbers) arrived.

On the day of *ping-yn* Che-hoang [Qin Shi Huangdi] died on the P'ing [Ping] terrace at Cha-k'ieou. The counsellor (Li) Se [Si], considering that the emperor had died far from the capital and fearing that the princes and the empire would make a revolution, kept the matter secret and did not announce the death. The coffin was placed in a covered vehicle.... They set

off…it was hot; bad smells emanated from the emperor's covered vehicle; then a decree ordered the officials of the retinue to put a che of salted fish in each chariot, in order to disguise the odour. The trip continued; they arrived at Hien-yang [Xianyang] by a direct route, and announced the death.

In the ninth month, they buried Che-hoang in Mount Li. At the start of his reign, Che-hoang had had Mount Li dug into and arranged. At that time he had united the whole empire and seven hundred thousand workers were sent there; they dug the soil down to water-level; they poured bronze and they brought the sarcophagus there; palaces (buildings for) all the administration, and marvellous utensils, jewels and rare objects were transported there and filled (the burial chamber). Artisans were ordered to make automatic crossbows and arrows; so that if someone had wanted to make a hole and get in (to the tomb) they would suddenly have fired at him. With mercury they made the hundred waterways, the Kiang [Jiang], the Ho [He], and the great ocean; machines made it flow from one to another. Above were depicted all the heavenly constellations; below lay the geographical representation of the earth. With *jen-yu* [seal] fat they made torches which, it was calculated, could not go out for a long time.… Very many people were put to death.… When the funeral was finished, and the central avenue leading to the burial had been hidden and blocked up, the gate to the outer entrance was dropped into place, and all those who had been employed as workers or artisans for hiding (the treasures) were shut inside; they could not get out. Grasses and plants were planted to make (the tomb) look like a mountain.

Historical Records of Sima Qian
1st century BC

Text and memory

Written documents and archaeological evidence provide much information about the past. In China the study of inscriptions, rubbings and research have helped to reveal even more, like a police investigation. For scholars, the decipherment of inscriptions is the means of establishing a link between past and present, and of passing from generation to generation the values and references of the past.

Written records and archaeological discoveries

Our knowledge of the early Chinese empire is drawn from two main sources: written records and archaeological discoveries. Unlike their Egyptian or Roman counterparts, the Chinese emperors left few imperial monuments above ground. Their lasting works were of a public nature such as the Great Wall, the Grand Canal, and the great irrigation systems of Sichuan. The use of wooden frameworks means that few pre-14th-century wooden buildings have survived, and all that remains of the great cities before that date are the rammed-earth-foundations of city walls, towers and terraces. Almost the only stone buildings are tombs, pagodas and bridges; stone monuments are limited to statuary and to memorial features placed on tombs.

This lack of visible remains is more than compensated for by the wealth of written texts. The Chinese have always attached great importance to the written word – an engraved inscription is valued far above any carved statue – and the modern Chinese pictorial script has recognizable links with the earliest hieroglyphs on bones from the 2nd millennium BC. The first Chinese historian, Sima Qian, wrote the *Historical Records* of early Chinese history in the 1st century BC and from that time onwards there exist Dynastic Histories. These were supplemented by local records which like the Dynastic Histories gave information under headings such as Biographies, Ritual and Ceremony (including official dress), Carriages and Monuments. The very wealth of information, however, brought a danger of historical distortion since it created the impression that all fields of activity were covered and that if something was not mentioned in the texts, it could not have been important. In fact, the scholar-officials of the court presented a selected version of events reflecting contemporary views; history was frequently reinterpreted to suit their rulers and large areas of activity were ignored as being beneath notice. For example, no textual references to the first emperor's great terracotta army have yet been found, and it was not until the 7th century AD, when the emperors became interested in fine quality porcelain, that China's best-known artifact – china – was mentioned in the texts.

Archaeological discoveries help to overcome these limitations. The ancient tradition of providing the dead with what they might need in the next world means that China's soil is a vast treasure house. There is no other country in the world where archaeological discoveries are taking place so fast and on such a scale as in China, discoveries which are continually expanding our knowledge of the past and reversing previously accepted ideas.

Ann Paludan
Chronicle of the Chinese Emperors:
The Reign-by-Reign Record of the Rulers
of Imperial China, 1998

The importance of inscriptions for our knowledge of Shang history

The Shang elite are commonly described as the rulers of the first East Asian state. Knowledge of the Shang-period political situation is gleaned from the inscriptions on the oracle bones. Such inscribed bones have so far been recovered from only two locations: the Late Shang site at Anyang and the contemporaneous predynastic Zhou 'capital' at Qishan.

The identification of protohistoric oracle bones in early 20th-century medicinal shops and the tracing of their source to Anyang is one of the most exciting and important archaeological detective stories of modern times. Their discovery led to the excavation of the Yinxu site at Anyang…with its oracle bone archives. The scapulae and plastrons had been carefully scraped down on the back side, and oval cavities about 1 cm long were hollowed out in rows; a heated metal rod was inserted into the cavities to produce cracks on the front surface. The cracks were then read by a diviner in answer to 'charges' put to him by the Shang king: was it auspicious to go hunting? Would the harvest be good? In contrast to Neolithic divination bones, the successful oracle bones were inscribed with the charges and then stored in an archive.

Some of the Shang inscriptions concern hunting or military campaigns and receipt of tribute; these can be looked upon as rudimentary administrative records and histories – material evidence of state organization. It is important to emphasize that almost all the information on Shang as a state derives from such inscriptions; other archaeological remains from the Shang period are of neither the quantity nor quality to reveal much about political organization at the time. And although other named groups mentioned in the inscriptional material are increasingly referred to as 'states' contemporaneous with the Shang state, they are difficult to identify archaeologically and lack detailed textual description.

Gina L. Barnes
China, Korea and Japan:
The Rise of Civilization in East Asia,
1993

A conversation with K. C. Chang

More than anyone else, Chang Kwang-chih (below) personifies the fragile link between the old and new generation, between China and Taiwan. For years, his work has constituted the primary source of information about Chinese archaeology for western researchers.

Chang Kwang-chih was born in 1931 in Beijing of a Taiwanese father and a Chinese mother. He lived and studied in Beijing until 1946, when his family returned to Taiwan. In 1950 he began his anthropology studies at Taiwan University with the famous Chinese anthropologist and specialist of Anyang, Li Chi. He left to study at Harvard in 1955, and later taught at Yale, and then at Harvard, where he is also curator at the Peabody Museum.

Helke Ferrie: *So you decided to study archaeology after high school?*

K. C. Chang: Yes. Taiwan University had then only recently established a department of anthropology and staffed it with people like Li Chi and others who had been excavators of Anyang. They were famous throughout China – everybody had heard their names – and I knew they were the greatest scholars in the university. I was 19 years old, and I felt I knew a little bit about anthropology and decided to register in that department....

H. F.: *How did you meet Li Chi for the first time?*

K. C. C.: Li Chi was the chairman of the department, and when I went to register he was manning the desk. I was the first one to register for archaeology. I still remember the moment. He looked at me over the top of his glasses and signed my registration card without a word.... Professor Shen Kang-po, the Dean of the College of Arts, who was next to sign my card, looked at me curiously and asked, 'Why did you decide on archaeology?' I was taken aback and spontaneously replied, 'Because it is fun.' He smiled and said, 'That's a good enough reason. Study hard. Do well.' And I began,....

H. F.: *So, it was Li Chi who trained you.*

K. C. C.: Li Chi and a number of other teachers. The traditional Chinese way of bringing up a scholar is basically an apprentice system, even today. Li Chi was different and a very enlightened person. I never felt that he owned me. He had studied at Harvard under Hooton, Tozzer and Dixon and received his doctorate here in 1923. He brought a western outlook on education to China.

H. F.: *How did that show in his behavior?*

K. C. C.: He did not regard himself as the master and his students as his disciples. His was a team spirit, a faculty spirit, where you try to take the best from each speciality....

H. F.: *Did Li Chi help to get you to Harvard?*

K. C. C.: Yes. He was teaching briefly in Mexico in 1954, when I was serving a mandatory year in the Taiwanese army....

H. F.: *What was your Ph.D. thesis on?*

K. C. C.: My thesis was a library thesis on prehistoric settlement patterns in China.

H. F.: *At that time, there was so little information – to do a thesis on settlement patterns must have taken some courage!*

K. C. C.: Courage isn't the right word. Rather: imprudent audacity! I didn't know any better. They allowed me to do a library thesis because China was closed to outsiders for field work and they felt I had had enough experience in digging by then, in France and in Taiwan.

H. F.: *What did your Ph.D. thesis contribute, at that time, to the research on settlement patterns?*

K. C. C.: I tried to introduce American methodology to the study of Chinese prehistory....

H. F.: *How did you begin teaching?*

K. C. C.: The first year after I got my degree I began teaching as an instructor here at Harvard. Li Chi wanted me to go back to Taiwan, but I didn't want to go back. In Chinese society young scholars have very little freedom of action and thought. The hierarchies are very rigid.... I always encourage my students to study at least one other area outside their specialization and to do so in depth. I myself did that early on also. I worked in France, and one of my earliest papers was on Neolithic social groupings in the New World. I feel you really need to know at least two very divergent areas very well. By knowing the other area you know your own even better....

H. F.: *Your approach goes against the trend of the New Archaeology toward identifying predictable universals....*

K. C. C.: I don't object to the search for universal laws. I think ultimately we may reach that point, but we have not reached it yet. For now, we must study each culture in detail, in depth, on its own terms, and in all its particulars....

H. F.: *You also wrote, 'it is the archaeologist's task to present the forms and fates of past choices as objectively as he can, so that in making decisions for the future, society will have lessons of the past.'... How does this continuity strike you, and do you consider it important?*

K. C. C.: The fact is that, unfortunately, traditional Chinese archaeology is virtually lost. There are really no Chinese students today who are trained in traditional scholarship.

But it is very important, because one needs to know the texts and history contemporary with the objects one is studying. The Northern Sung [Song] was the dynasty most favourable to the growth of archaeological thinking. All the great bronze catalogues were done during the Sung. But traditional antiquarianism is no longer taught in schools. You have to go to an archaeology department of a university to learn something about it. I still got the tail-end of that traditional education [1931–46], but for the generations after me the continuity was interrupted – it was really eliminated along with the general attempt to destroy many traditions of Chinese society. Mao wanted to create a new China. He had some dreams about changing the Chinese mind and bringing China out of the feudal era to a more western present, but I don't think he understood the West very well. The Cultural Revolution resulted primarily in a tragic destruction – but that is a long story....

H. F.: *Do you find that the application of the Chinese-Marxist periodization scheme of primitive, slave, feudal, and capitalist stages of social development does a lot of violence to the archaeological evidence?*

K. C. C.: I used to be a believer in the Marxist periodization scheme. That was because of Guo Muruo's great work on the Shang bronzes…but you see, once I began to examine the evidence carefully, I found that the Marxist periodization scheme just does not work. I don't find that change can be attributed to the power of production as the Marxist scheme demands, with the result that the relations of production change accordingly. In early China, in the Longshan, Yangshao, and the Three Dynasties right up to the beginning

of the Iron Age, I just don't find any change in the forces of production. There just is no appreciable change of technology. Marxist historians, especially in the '50s and until Mao's death, looked for signs of technological change to fit their doctrine, but they just didn't look at the evidence. In their papers there is no effort to use the evidence to support what is being said....

H. F.: *For many years now you have been sometimes the only link between the western and Chinese archaeological communities. Can you tell us something about your visit to China as a member of the American palaeoanthropology delegation in 1975?...*

K. C. C.: Our delegation was very carefully managed. The archaeologists we really wanted to talk to were usually unavailable or busy with the harvest. We could not really ask any of the questions we wanted to ask, and we were given completely fictitious figures regarding production prior to Liberation and after, prior to the Cultural Revolution and after, and so on. But I went back on my own in 1977, and that was a completely different experience. You see, Mao Tse-tung [Mao Zedong] had died in 1976, in the same year of that terrible earthquake there. But the most dramatic change came by 1980. That's when everything finally loosened up. We were able to talk freely with each other, and I learned that Chinese archaeologists had not really assimilated Marxist doctrine. When you read their articles, you find that usually only the introductory paragraph and a portion of the conclusion will pay homage to Marxist doctrine with some quotation from Marx or Engels. The rest of the article is real archaeology, actual facts. In conversation with them it was the same.

H. F.: *Were they open to discussing theory with you?*

K. C. C.: Before Liberation, theory was not very important. Even Li Chi was not interested in theory. Theory was never really explicit. Then Mao came, and as long as he was alive there was no theory permitted except the Marxist one. But I strongly doubt that any of the Chinese archaeologists actually believed it. They conformed to the national policy because they had to. They were also unable to design any methodology that tested theory – you don't have to if the Marxist theory is already accepted. This was really too bad, because from 1949 on method and theory stagnated in China. They never questioned the validity of assumptions about matriarchal stages of society or any other parts of Engels' scheme. But because Chinese archaeologists were prevented from going through the development Americans experienced with the New Archaeology, they did not have the opportunity to experience what happens when theoretical questions generate a multiplicity of methods which produce rich and relevant data....

H. F.: *In 1986 and 1987 you became a guest professor at Xiamen and Beijing universities. Did you find teaching Chinese students a very different experience?*

K. C. C.: Dramatically different! Western students like to form independent opinions. The undergraduate students at Harvard and Yale especially cut through to the core of an issue very quickly and never accept a teacher's opinion blindly. They are critical of any established wisdom and

want to be better than their professors. And this is essential for good scholarship. On the down side, they often lack patience. They want quick answers. The Chinese students are the exact reverse: they are very patient, and they accept whatever the teacher says. They are rarely critical, and they want to be as good as the teacher but dare not hope for more. In graduate school a student's program is controlled totally by one professor, who is his master. I have given the Chinese universities a hard time by repeatedly criticizing this traditional educational approach.... Their educational system handicaps archaeology, especially because they only study China. I have told them, 'You cannot do good archaeology if you do not study the rest of the world as well and give the student freedom to discover new ideas.'...

H. F.: *At the end of your textbook you wrote that we are entering the Golden Age of Chinese archaeology.*

K. C. C.: Yes, that is very true, but I am referring to potential which is not yet fully realized. There is so much to be discovered in China!

From 'A Conversation with K. C. Chang' with Helke Ferrie for the journal *Current Anthropology*, volume 36, number 2, April 1995, published by the University of Chicago Press

PERIOD/DYNASTY	DATES	PHASE, CULTURE
		NEOLITHIC
South-east China	c. 10000–5000 BC	
Central-south China	c. 6000 BC	Pengtoushan
Central-north China	c. 5500–4900 BC	Cishan-Peiligang
	c. 4800–2500 BC	Yangshao
South-east China	c. 5000–4770 BC	Hemudu
Eastern China (Shandong, Anhui, Jiangsu, Henan)	c. 4500–2500 BC	Dawenkou
North-east China	c. 3800–2700 BC	Hongshan
North-west China	c. 3500–1500 BC	Majiayao (Majiayao, Banshan, Machang phases)
South-east China	c. 3000–2000 BC	Liangzhu
Eastern China and central plain	c. 2500–1700 BC	Longshan
		BRONZE AGE
XIA (C. 2000–1600 BC)	c. 1700–1500 BC	Erlitou
SHANG (C. 1600–1050 BC)	c. 1600–1400 BC	Erligang
	c. 1400–1050 BC	Anyang
	c. 1200–1000 BC	Hunan Jiangxi Sichuan

Sites	World events
NEOLITHIC	
Caves and shell mounds (Guangxi, Guangdong, Jiangxi)	
Pengtoushan (Hunan). No doubt the oldest cultivated rice	
Cishan (Henan, discovered 1976). Peiligang (Hebei)	
Yangshao (Henan, discovered 1921), Banpo (Shaanxi, excavated 1954–7), Dahecun (Henan, excavated 1970s)	
Hemudu (Zhejiang, discovered 1973)	
Dawenkou (Shandong, discovered 1959)	4000 BC: megalithic culture in the West
Hongshanhou (discovered 1938), Dongshanzui and Niuheliang (discovered 1981) in Liaoning	
Zhujiazhai (discovered 1923), Liuwan (excavated 1974–8) in Qinghai	
Liangzhu (discovered 1936) and Sidun (Jiangsu), Fanshan (Zhejiang)	3000 BC: cuneiform writing at Sumer
Chengziyai (Shandong), Pingliangtai (Henan, discovered 1979)	2530 BC: the sphinx at Giza
ARCHAIC ROYALTY	
Erlitou near Yanshi (Henan): palace and first bronze vessels (discovered 1958). The site contains pre-Shang and early Shang levels	2000–1800 BC: construction of the first Minoan palaces on Crete
Erligang-Zhengzhou (Henan): fortified city, probably ancient Shang capital (excavated 1950s)	1500 BC: Stonehenge in Britain
Panlongcheng and Lijiazui (Hubei): fortified city and tombs	
Anyang (Henan), last Shang capital comprising a whole series of sites: Xiaotun (palatial site), Houjiazhuang and Xibeigang (11 cruciform royal tombs), Wuguancun (large tomb and sacrificial victims), Dasikongcun (chariot burials), tomb of Fu Hao (c. 1200 BC), the only undisturbed royal tomb (discovered 1976)	1279–1213 BC: reign of Ramesses II
Ningxiang (Hunan): southern-style bronzes (excavated 1960s)	1250 BC: Trojan War
Wucheng and Xin'gan (Jiangxi): tomb of Dayangzhou (excavated 1970s)	
Sanxingdui (Sichuan): city and sacrificial pits (excavated 1986)	1000 BC: reign of Solomon

PERIOD/DYNASTY	DATES	PHASE, CULTURE
ZHOU (C. 1050–221 BC)	Western Zhou (c. 1050–771 BC)	
	Eastern Zhou (770–221 BC)	Spring and Autumn (770–475 BC
		Warring States (475–221 BC)

IRON AGE

QIN (221–207 BC)	

Sites	World events
Qishan, Futeng, Baoji (Shaanxi)	1050 BC: destruction of Mycenae
Zhuangbai near Fufeng (Shaanxi): cache of bronzes, c. 880 BC (discovered 1976)	
Shangcunling (Henan): burials of the state of Guo (excavated since 1990)	800 BC: composition of the *Iliad*
End of the Western Zhou (9th–8th centuries BC)	
Tianma-Qucun (Shanxi): burials of the lords of Jin	753 BC: foundation of Rome
Pingdingshan (Henan): tombs of the state of Ying (excavated 1990)	600 BC: foundation of Marseilles
Houma (Shanxi): capital of the state of Jin and foundry (discovered 1956)	563 BC: birth of Buddha
Liyu (Shanxi): bronzes of the 5th–6th centuries (discovered 1923)	551 BC: birth of Confucius
Jiangling (Hubei): capital of the kingdom of Chu	
Leigudun (Hubei): tomb of Marquis Yi of Zeng, who died in 433 BC (discovered 1977)	
Wangshan, Mashan, Zidanku (Hubei): cemeteries of the Chu culture (4th–3rd centuries BC)	c. 300 BC: Parthian empire in Persia
Pingshan (Hebei): tombs of the kings of Zhongshan (4th century; discovered 1974)	
Jincun (Henan): 3rd century BC (discovered 1928)	
Guweicun, Henan (discovered 1951)	
IMPERIAL CHINA	
Great Wall	
Fengxiang (Shaanxi)	
Xianyang (Shaanxi): Qin capital from 350 to 207 BC	
Lintong (Shaanxi): tumulus of Qin Shi Huangdi and pits of warriors and horses (discovered 1974)	218–201 BC: Second Punic War
Bronze quadrigas (discovered 1980)	

PERIOD/DYNASTY	DATES	PHASE, CULTURE
HAN (206 BC–AD 220)	Western Han (206 BC–AD 9)	
	Xin (AD 9–25)	
	Eastern Han (AD 25–220)	

SITES	WORLD EVENTS
Chang'an (Shaanxi): capital	
Yangjiawan (Shaanxi): tomb with funerary figures	
Mawangdui near Changsha (Hunan): tomb of the Marquise of Dai, who died c. 168 BC (discovered 1971)	
Yangling (Shaanxi): pit annexe to the mausoleum of the emperor Jingdi, who died in 141 BC (excavated 1989)	146 BC: destruction of Carthage
Canton: tomb of the second king of Nanyue, who died in 122 BC (discovered 1983)	100 BC: birth of Caesar
Mancheng (Hebei): tombs of the Western Han prince Liu Sheng and his wife Dou Wan, who died in 113 and 104 BC respectively (discovered 1968)	41 BC: meeting of Antony and Cleopatra
Maoling (Shaanxi): tombs of the emperor Wudi, who died in 87 BC, and General Huo Qubing, who died in 117 BC	29–19 BC: Virgil composes the *Aeneid*
Luoyang (Henan): capital and tombs of stamped bricks	AD 64: fire of Rome
Mizhi (Shaanxi): tomb dated 107	
Wu Liang (Shandong): small funerary chamber of the Wu family (c. 150). First mentioned in the 11th century, study by Chavannes in 1875	AD 70: destruction of the temple of Jerusalem
Helinger (Inner Mongolia): tomb of a colonel who died around 170 (discovered 1972)	AD 79: destruction of Pompeii
Chengdu (Sichuan): rock tombs, funerary figurines	
Leitai near Wuwei (Gansu): tomb of a general and his wife (c. 186–219)	AD 165: persecution of Christians at Rome
Loulan and Niya (Xinjiang)	

HISTORICAL LANDMARKS

Imperial China

221–207 BC Qin dynasty

206 BC–AD 220 Han dynasty

220–581 Period of the Three Kingdoms (220–280) and the Six Dynasties

581–618 Sui dynasty

618–907 Tang dynasty

907–60 Five Dynasties

907–1125 Liao dynasty (Manchurian dynasty)

960–1279 Song dynasty

1279–1368 Yuan dynasty (Mongolian dynasty)

1368–1644 Ming dynasty (restoration of the imperial tradition)

1644–1911 Qing dynasty (Manchurian dynasty)

1840–42 Opium War

1850–64 The Taiping rebellion, a movement that wanted to oust the Manchu from power

1860 Sacking of the Summer Palace, Beijing, by Anglo-French troops. The foreign powers imposed 'unequal treaties' on China, which was forced to open up to foreigners. Russians, Germans, British and French shared China between them

1890–1914 Rivalries between the great powers

1894–95 Sino-Japanese war, lost by China. The Japanese reach Port Arthur

1896 Russia builds the Trans-Manchurian railway

1900 The members of a secret Chinese society, the Boxers, besiege the Legation Quarter in Beijing where foreigners gathered. They are massacred. China has to pay heavy compensation to the foreign powers

1905 Empress Cixi has to consent to some reforms. Dr Sun Yatsen (Sun Wen) leads a revolutionary movement with the aim of overthrowing the dynasty, fighting against foreigners and putting a modern government in place. The first nationalist party (Guomindang) is founded

1911 So-called 'bourgeois' revolution. Disintegration of central power. Fall of the dynasty

Chinese Republic (1912–49)

1912 Proclamation of the Chinese Republic at Nanjing, with Sun Wen as president. Emperor Puyi abdicates. Sun Wen was soon replaced by Yuan Shikai, chief of the northern forces. He settled in Beijing, and tried to restore the empire to his advantage, but failed. There followed a period of chaos. The Japanese tried to settle in China

1917–28 Between anarchy and reconquest. Struggle between the 'warlords'

1919 The treaty of Paris, unfavourable to China, results in a protest movement by Chinese students

1921 Foundation of the Chinese Communist Party, in which Mao Zedong takes part. Sun Wen becomes president of the Southern Chinese Republic proclaimed at Canton

1925 Nationalists and Communists become allies to try and take power over the whole territory. Death of Sun Wen. Jiang Jieshi, a young general who had returned from Moscow, directs operations. Agrarian reform. Russian influence on China

1927 Deterioration of relationship between the two parties. Jiang Jieshi allies himself with the Nationalists in the North. The Guomindang is in power (until 1935). The Communists, who have to go into hiding, settle in the south and have a guerrilla force

1931 The Japanese begin their invasion of the north-east, and notably in Manchuria, which becomes their base for attacks in northern China. In the south, the Reds found the first Soviet Republic. Mao is elected provisional president, but another revolutionary, Zhou Enlai, was pre-eminent for a while

1932 Manchuria is proclaimed independent and takes the name of Manchukuo

1934–5 'Long March' of the Communists' Red Army from Jiangxi to Shaanxi and Yenan to escape the Nationalist troops of the Guomindang. Red China is constructed (1935–45)

1937–45 Sino-Japanese war (ends with Japanese capitulation)

1947 Resumption of the civil war in the north between Jiang Jieshi and the Communists. Gradual collapse of the Goumindang

1949 The Communists take control of China. Mao Zedong proclaims the People's Republic of China on 1 October. Jiang Jieshi goes into exile in Taiwan with the Nationalist government

People's Republic of China (since 1949)

1966–76 'Cultural Revolution' instigated by Mao Zedong to regain control of the Party

1976 Death of Zhou Enlai and of Mao

FURTHER READING

Andersson, J. G., 'Prehistory of the Chinese', *Bulletin of the Museum of Far Eastern Antiquities*, XV, 1943

Bagley, R. W., *Shang Ritual Bronzes in the Arthur M. Sackler Collections*, 1987

Barnes, Gina L., *China, Korea and Japan: The Rise of Civilization in East Asia*, 1993

Bunker, Emma C., *Ancient Bronzes of the Eastern Eurasian Steppes from the Arthur M. Sackler Collections*, 1997

Capon, Edmund, *Art and Archaeology in China*, 1977

—, and William MacQuitty, *Princes of Jade*, 1973

Chang, K. C., *The Archaeology of Ancient China*, 4th ed., 1986

—, *Early Chinese Civilization: Anthropological Perspectives*, 1976

—, *Shang Civilization*, 1980

— (ed.), *Studies of Shang Archaeology*, 1986

Cotterell, Arthur, *The First Emperor of China*, 1981

Ebrey, Patricia B., *The Cambridge Illustrated History of China*, 1996

Elisseeff, Danielle, and Vadime Elisseeff, *New Discoveries in China*, 1983

Falkenhausen, Lothar von, *Suspended Music: Chime Bells in the Culture of Bronze Age China*, 1993

Fong, Wen (ed.), *The Great Bronze Age of China: An Exhibition from the People's Republic of China*, 1980

Gernet, Jacques, *A History of Chinese Civilization*, trans. J. R. Foster, 1982

Hook, Brian (ed.), *The Cambridge Encyclopaedia of China*, 1990

Hsu, C. Y., and Katheryn M. Linduff, *Western Chou Civilization*, 1988

Keightley, David N., *Sources of Shang History: The Oracle-Bone Inscriptions of Bronze Age China*, 1978

— (ed.), *The Origins of Chinese Civilization*, 1983

Lawton, Thomas (ed.), *New Perspectives on Chu Culture during the Eastern Zhou Period*, 1991

Lee, Sherman E., *A History of Far Eastern Art*, 5th ed., 1997

Li Chi, *Anyang: A Chronicle of the Discovery, Excavation and Reconstruction of the Ancient Capital of the Shang Dynasty*, 1977

Li Xueqin, *Eastern Zhou and Qin Civilizations*, trans. K. C. Chang, 1985

Nelson, Sarah M. (ed.), *The Archaeology of Northeast China, Beyond the Great Wall*, 1995

Paladun, Ann, *The Chinese Spirit Road – the Classical Tradition of Stone Tomb Sculpture*, 1991

—, *Chronicle of the Chinese Emperors: The Reign-by-Reign Record of the Rulers of Imperial China*, 1998

Pirazzoli-t'Serstevens, Michèle (ed.), *The Han Dynasty*, 1982

Rawson, Jessica, *Ancient China: Art and Archaeology*, 1980

—, *Chinese Jade, from the Neolithic to the Qing*, 1995

—, *Western Zhou Ritual Bronzes from the Arthur M. Sackler Collections*, 1990

— (ed.), *The British Museum Book of Chinese Art*, 1992

Segalen, Victor, A. Gilbert de Voisins, and J. Lartigue, *Mission archéologique en Chine, 1914 et 1917*, 2 vols., 1923–4

Sickman, Laurence, and Alexander Soper, *The Art and Architecture of China*, 1978

Tregear, Mary, *Chinese Art*, 1997

Twitchett, Denis, and John F. Fairbank (eds.), *The Cambridge History of China*, 1978–86

Watson, Burton, *Records of the Grand Historian of China*, trans. Burton Watson, 1961

Watson, William, *Art of Dynastic China*, 1981

Whitfield, Roderick (ed.), *The Problem of Meaning in Early Chinese Ritual Bronzes*, 1993

LIST OF ILLUSTRATIONS

CHAPTER 2

CHAPTER 3

CHAPTER 4

CHAPTER 5

pit, mausoleum of Qin Shi Huangdi at Lintong in Shaanxi, Qin dynasty. Photograph
99a Head of terracotta warrior being excavated, soldier pit, mausoleum of Qin Shi Huangdi at Lintong in Shaanxi, Qin dynasty. Photograph
99b Detail of a terracotta warrior's hand, soldier pit, mausoleum of Qin Shi Huangdi at Lintong in Shaanxi, Qin dynasty. Photograph

CHAPTER 6

100 Funerary figurine, annexe-pit to the mausoleum of Emperor Jingdi (Yanling) near Xianyang in Shaanxi, excavated 1989, period of Western Han. Moulded red clay. Photograph
101 Exorcist or guardian, discovered in 1965 near Chengdu in Sichuan, period of the Eastern Han. Funerary statuette in terracotta, height 44 cm (17⅜"). Sichuan Provincial Museum, Chengdu
102 *Lian* toilet box, tomb no. 1 of Mawangdui (Changsha) in Hunan, period of the Western Han (shortly after 168 BC), excavated 1972. Painted lacquer on core of hemp and silk
102–3 Painted silk banner, tomb no. 1 of Mawangdui (Changsha) in Hunan, period of the Western Han (shortly after 168 BC), excavated 1972. Height 2.05 m (6¾'). Hunan Provincial Museum, Changsha
103 Funerary statuettes, tomb no. 1 of Mawangdui (Changsha) in Hunan, period of the Western Han (shortly after 168 BC). Carved and painted wood, height c. 43 cm (16⅞")
104 Tiered pit, tomb no. 1 of Mawangdui (Changsha) in Hunan in the course of excavation, period of the Western Han (shortly after 168 BC). Photograph
105a Dismantling the funerary chamber in tomb no. 1 of Mawangdui (Changsha) in Hunan, period of the Western Han (shortly after 168 BC). Photograph
105b The third inner coffin of the Marquise of Dai, tomb no. 1 of Mawangdui (Changsha) in Hunan, excavated 1972, period of the Western Han (shortly after 168 BC). Wood with polychrome decoration on a base of red lacquer. Photograph
106 Unearthing a lacquer vessel, tomb no. 1 of Mawangdui (Changsha) in Hunan, excavated 1972, period of the Western Han (shortly after 168 BC). Photograph
107l Mummy of the Marquise of Dai, tomb no. 1 of Mawangdui (Changsha) in Hunan, excavated 1972, period of the Western Han (shortly after 168 BC). Photograph

107r *Fang* vessel, tomb no. 1 of Mawangdui (Changsha) in Hunan, excavated 1972, period of the Western Han (shortly after 168 BC). Carved and lacquered wood. Hunan Provincial Museum, Changsha
108a Eastern face of the lintel and the pediment separating the vestibule and the funerary chamber, tomb no. 61 of Luoyang in Henan, period of the Western Han (c. 48–47 BC). Hollow painted bricks
108b East-west axonometric view of tomb no. 61 of Luoyang in Henan, period of the Western Han (c. 48–47 BC)
109a, 109c, 109b Zoomorphic sculptures in granite associated with the tomb of General Huo Qubing (140–117 BC) near Maoling (Xi'an) in Shaanxi
110ar Watchtower, Kucha region in Xinjiang, Han period. Photograph
110br Stag with the beak of a bird of prey, tomb of Nalin'gaotu (Shenmu) in Shaanxi, late 4th century BC. Hair ornament in gold, height 11.5 cm (4½")
110l, 111a, 111b Funerary figurines in terracotta, annexe-pit to the mausoleum of the emperor Jingdi (died 141 BC) at Yanling near Xianyang (Shaanxi). Height 60 cm (23⅝")
112 The tomb of Liu Sheng at Mancheng in Hebei, period of the Western Han (113 BC). Photograph
112–3 Shroud, headrest and stoppers, tomb of Liu Sheng at Mancheng in Hebei, period of the Western Han (113 BC). Jade, gold and gilded bronze, length 188 cm (74"). Photograph. Hebei Provincial Museum
113a Jade amulet, period of the Western Han. Musée Cernuschi, Paris
113c Perforated jade disk with decoration of dragon and phoenix unfurling in scrolls, tomb of the second king of Nanyue, who died in 122 BC. Museum of the tomb of the king of Nanyue, Canton
114–5 Rubbing of the decoration of a chiselled stone lintel, tomb no. 4 of Mizhi in the north of Shaanxi, period of the Eastern Han (AD 107)
114 Vaulted tomb of brick, district of Huaiyang in Henan, period of the Eastern Han. Photograph
115 Hanging lampbearer, end of the Eastern Han (2nd century). Bronze, height 29 cm (11⅛"). Hunan Provincial Museum, Changsha
116–7 Horses, tomb of Helinger in Inner Mongolia, period of the Eastern Han (c. 170). Mural painting. Museum of Chinese History, Beijing

DOCUMENTS

INDEX OF SITES

GENERAL INDEX

ACKNOWLEDGMENTS

The publisher would like to thank: Jean-Pierre Drège, administrator of the EFEO (Ecole Française d'Extrême Orient); Mrs Wang-Toutaint, researcher at the EFEO; Gilles Béguin, chief curator of the Musée Cernuschi; M. Macouin, chief curator of the library of the Musée des Arts Asiatiques Guimet; Marianne Verdeaux, librarian at the Musée Cernuschi; Yan Delorme and Yong Jin, researchers at the CNRS (Centre National de Recherche Scientifique).

PHOTO CREDITS

Academia Sinica archives, Taipei 12, 30a, 31, 52, 52–3, 60–1, 61. All rights reserved 32r, 70–1, 76l, 76c, 88, 91a, 108a. British Library, London 14b, 15b, 22–3. British Museum, London 71. Bureau representing Taipei in France, Paris 32l. China Pictorial Publications, Beijing front cover (background), 33r, 86. Cultural Relics Publishing House, Beijing front cover (foreground), back cover, spine, 1–9, 26, 36, 38a, 40bl, 40br, 41l, 41r, 42bl, 42br, 43, 44l, 48, 49a, 49b, 50, 54b, 55b, 58–9, 60a, 62b, 64bl, 64br, 66a, 66b, 67l, 67r, 68, 73, 74, 81a, 81b, 82–3, 83b, 87a, 87b, 94–5a, 94–5b, 96b, 96–7, 97b, 100, 101, 105b, 107r, 112–3, 113c, 115, 118–9, 120–1, 121, 122–3, 124–5, 126a, 126b. Current Anthropology, University of Chicago Press 138. Dagli-Orti, Paris 99b. Explorer Archives, Paris 80. Gallimard archives, Paris 18–9, 23, 38–9, 39, 58, 70, 93b. Gamma, Paris 35, 99a. Gamma/Berg, Paris 128. Hao Jinlan, Beijing 30b, 72b, 72ar, 73al. Harvard University, Arthur M. Sackler Museum, Cambridge, Massachusetts 84–5. Patrick Léger/Gallimard 13, 16a, 16b, 16–7, 17, 20b, 25a, 27a, 27b, 110br, 110l, 111a, 111b, 131, 147a. Metropolitan Museum of Art, New York 56–7. Roland and Sabrina Michaud, Paris 44–5, 82, 83a, 89, 116–7, 118. Museum of Far Eastern Antiquities, Stockholm 25b, 133. National Geographic Society, Washington, D. C. 98r. National Museum of Ethnography, Stockholm 20–1. National Palace Museum, Taipei 14a. Picture library of the Musées de la Ville de Paris 11, 51, 113a, 119, 124a, 124b, 146a, 146bl, 146br. Private collection 20a, 38b, 47, 54a, 55a, 59, 60b, 65ar, 65b, 76–7, 78–9a, 78–9b, 79, 90a, 90b, 108b, 109a, 109c, 109b, 114–5, 125, 127, 134–5, 142br, 143, 144c, 144b, 147b. Private collection, Corinne Francfort 34, 34–5, 46, 85, 93a. Rapho/Yamashita, Paris 46–7. Réunion des Musées Nationaux/Thierry Ollivier, Paris 15a. Réunion des Musées Nationaux, Paris 33l, 40bc, 53, 69. Robert Harding Picture Library, London 98l, 110ar. Sackler Museum, Beijing 37, 44b, 75. Shanghai Museum 77, 91b, 142bl, 144a. Teilhard de Chardin Foundation, Paris 24, 28, 28–9, 29. Xinhua/Gamma, Paris 62a, 63, 102, 102–3, 104, 114. Xinhua Photo Agency, Beijing 40r, 42a, 65a, 72a, 92, 92–3, 103, 105a, 106, 107l, 112, 129.

TEXT CREDITS

Grateful acknowledgment is made for use of material from the following work:
(pp. 138–41) 'A Conversation with K. C. Chang' with Helke Ferrie, *Current Anthropology*, volume 36, number 2, April 1995, published by the University of Chicago Press, © 1995 by The Wenner-Gren Foundation for Anthropological Research. All rights reserved 0011-3204/95/3602-0005$1.00. Reprinted by permission of *Current Anthropology*, USA, the University of Chicago Press, USA, and Helke Ferrie.

Corinne Debaine-Francfort,
an archaeologist and Sinologist,
is a researcher with the CNRS.
A specialist in the protohistory of north-west China,
she is a member of a team carrying out research
on Central Asia. She has taken part in various
archaeological expeditions in this region,
and in the first Sino-foreign excavation
to be authorized by China since 1949.
Since 1995 she has been co-director
of the Franco-Chinese archaeological
mission to Xinjiang.

For Vincent and Justine

Translated from the French by Paul G. Bahn

For Harry N. Abrams, Inc.
Eve Sinaiko, editorial

Library of Congress Cataloging-in-Publication Data

Debaine-Francfort, Corinne.
[La redécouverte de la Chine ancienne. English]
The search for ancient china / Corinne Debaine-Francfort.
     p.   cm. — (Discoveries)
Includes bibliographical references and index.
ISBN 0–8109–2850–7 (pbk.)
1. China—Antiquities. 2. Archaeology—China. 3. China—
Civilization. 4. China—History—To 221 B.C. 5. China—History—
Han dynasty, 202 B.C.–220 A.D.   I. Title. II. Series: Discoveries
(New York, N.Y.)
DS715.D4313   1999
931—dc21

                                                             99–10996

Printed and bound in Italy by Editoriale Lloyd